Big Bend
Tales

Big Bend
Tales

Mike Cox

Published by The History Press
Charleston, SC 29403
www.historypress.net

Images are from the author's collection unless otherwise noted.

First published 2011

Manufactured in the United States

ISBN 978.1.60949.330.1

Library of Congress Cataloging-in-Publication Data

Cox, Mike, 1948-
Big Bend tales / Mike Cox.
p. cm.
ISBN 978-1-60949-330-1
1. Big Bend Region (Tex.)--History--Anecdotes. 2. Big Bend Region (Tex.)--History, Local--Anecdotes. 3. Big Bend Region (Tex.)--Social life and customs--Anecdotes. 4. Big Bend Region (Tex.)--Biography--Anecdotes. I. Title.
F392.B54C69 2011
976.4'93--dc23
2011027999

Notice: The information in this book is true and complete to the best of our knowledge. It is offered without guarantee on the part of the author or The History Press. The author and The History Press disclaim all liability in connection with the use of this book.

Contents

Acknowledgements 9
Introduction 11

Indians
The Comanche Trail 13
The Legend of Indian Emily 16

Soldiers
Zenas Bliss's High Country Scout 19
Camp Pena Colorado Outlasted Fort Davis 21
"That Added Zest of Danger" 24

Critters
The Davis Mountain Grizzly 28
Taps for Louie 32

Drawing the Map
In the Beginning, There Was Bexar 34
Alpine Courthouse Once Served Three Counties 36

Contents

Ghost Towns

Lindsey City 39

Tesnus 40

Progress City 44

Landmarks

Ernst Tinaja 47

San Esteban Springs 50

Alpine's Holland Hotel 53

Rancho Valle de la Cienga 57

Big Bend Promoters

Touring a Future Park with a One-Armed Ranger 61

Jack Hoxie Saw Fort Davis as "Hollywood" East 64

Getting There and Back

"The Sun Has Riz, the Sun Has Set" 68

McDonald Observatory VIPs Trapped in Orbit 70

Johnny Newell's Road Logs 74

Laughing Matters

Just a "Little Side Show" 78

Here's Spit in Your Eye 80

Law and Disorder

Bud Newman and His Gang 83

Why Bill Taylor Disappeared 85

"Harry, Don't Kill Me!" 87

Harvey Hughes's Short Literary Career 91

The Lady in Chartreuse 94

Contents

Characters

The Hunchback of Ojinaga 98

Elmo Johnson 100

Three Big Bend Women

The Queen of the Pecos 104

Lizzie Closson 107

The Lady Shot a Lion 110

Here's to Your Health

Galloping Consumption 114

Flora's Tree 117

Mysteries

A Mountain Mystery 120

The Wonderful Boy 122

El Viejo Gringo 124

The Man Under the Black Fedora 129

Chroniclers

Before Twitter, "Coo-er" Carried the News 133

J. Frank Dobie in the Big Bend 136

Low Man on the Totem Pole Comes to Alpine 138

About the Author 143

Acknowledgements

Once again, a fatherly shout-out for my daughter Hallie Cox, who scanned the images used in this book. She also used her computer and artistic skills to touch up several of the illustrations. And a special thanks to several Big Bend folks who were particularly helpful during the research and writing of this book: Melleta R. Bell, senior archivist at Sul Ross State University's Archives of the Big Bend; Center for Big Bend Studies archaeologist Roger Boren and center director Andy Cloud; historian and former West Texas sheriff Glenn Willeford; MacGuire Ranch foreman David Williams; and writer/history buff Jim Wilson (also a former sheriff.)

Introduction

It's hard to believe, thinking back, how much mental effort it must have taken me not to look excited the first time my editor on the *San Angelo Standard-Times* said that he needed me to go to Alpine to handle several story assignments.

"You're going to pay me to go to the Big Bend?" Of course, I only thought that; I didn't say it. In the 1960s, touchy-feely management techniques had not yet entered the newsroom. The boss was the boss. Besides, not yet even nineteen, I had to try to act as worldly as possible. Betraying my delight in getting to travel to Alpine in a company vehicle and with expenses paid would not look good.

I had passed through Alpine several times, traveling with my grandparents from Austin to El Paso and back, but other than a visit to old Fort Davis in 1955 and again nine years later, I had not spent much time in the Texas high country until the San Angelo daily hired me in 1967. Happily, I have been back many times since then, variously on someone else's nickel or mine, but never often enough.

While Alpine, Fort Davis and Marfa are definitely part of the Big Bend, the three county seats are really only the scenic gateways to the magnificent country that stretches one hundred miles and more to the south—the mountains and vast desert inside the great bend of the Rio Grande that gave the region its name. In doing research for this book, I ran across this hard-to-improve-on early description, written by former Texas Ranger Andrew Jackson Sowell at his camp in the Chinati Mountains in the winter of 1918:

"This is a Big Bend country sure enough. From a short distance below El Paso the Rio Grande curves around to Langtry like a bent bow for 200 miles or more, the Southern Pacific Railroad being the string to the bow."

Big Bend Tales is a collection of forty-two true tales about Big Bend people and places, from the great Comanche Trail that cut through the region to the story of an eccentric big-time author who, late in his life, decided to abandon the man-made canyons of New York for a mountainside home overlooking Alpine. As with *West Texas Tales*, my first book in this series, I have focused on lesser-known or never-published stories. Given my love of the Big Bend, it was a fun book to put together, my only frustration being that a lot of good stories had to be left untold.

I'm not the first person in my family to be fascinated with the Big Bend. My late grandfather, L.A. Wilke, also a newspaperman turned freelance writer, spent some time in the Big Bend in the 1920s and '30s when it was far less known—and visited—than it is today.

On our way back to Austin from a visit with my aunt and uncle in El Paso in the summer of 1964, I talked Granddad into making a slight detour to Fort Davis so I could meet writer-historian Barry Scobee and get a copy of his latest book, *Fort Davis Texas 1583–1960*. Granddad had known Scobee for years and easily got me an audience with him. Beyond that, he shelled out six dollars for the book. Long out of print, it's now worth several hundred dollars, but bearing this inscription, to me it's priceless: "Autographed with pleasure for Mike Cox, an up and coming young historian, to whom, Best wishes, Barry Scobee at old Fort Davis Aug. 11, 1964."

No one could accuse me of being a young historian anymore, but at least I don't have to hide my excitement any time I get an opportunity to visit the Big Bend.

Indians

The Comanche Trail

Climbing to well-known vantage points in the mountains, the lookouts cut brush, stack it and begin their vigil. Each night, as they look anxiously to the northeast, the September moon rises later and larger, finally hanging as big as a cartwheel over the rugged peaks of the Big Bend country. In the full moon's silver light, the watchers can see to the far horizon.

One night, the northernmost sentinel makes the first sighting. In the distance, where the night before there had been nothing, it seems as if the stars have settled on the ground—a constellation of tiny, flickering lights. Campfires.

Quickly, the lookout ignites his greasewood pyre, and flames shoot into the clear, dry air. The watcher on the next peak sees the fire and lights his brush pile to alert the lookout on the next height. Soon, all across the Big Bend, down to the Rio Grande and on into Mexico, the word has spread: *the Comanches are coming.*

Beginning in the 1700s—after they acquired horses and learned to use them so well that they came to be called the finest light cavalry in the world—Comanche warriors annually raided south of the Rio Grande under a full September moon, when the grass grew high and the water holes stood full. The Comanches called it the time of the Mexican Moon. The people on the frontier of Texas and northern Mexico called it the time of the Comanche Moon.

Comanche Springs at Fort Stockton was an important water hole on the Comanche Trail until the soldiers came.

The Comanche Trail was west Texas's first major transportation route—a long, dusty trace dug deep over the generations by thousands of hooves, dampened each year with tears and blood. From what is now Kansas in the upper reaches of the land once known as Comancheria, the trail—actually a series of trails, followed by various bands—led one thousand miles to the south, plunging like a Comanche lance straight into Mexico's poorly defended northern frontier.

Before the Mexicans, before the American soldiers and surveyors, before the gold-seeking forty-niners, before the cattlemen and the farmers, the Comanche Trail cut across the land from plains to desert to mountain passes. For more than a century, this trail—the historical equivalent to today's interstate highway—amounted to one of the longest commercial routes in North America.

The raids began when the area south of the Rio Grande still formed the northern frontier of New Spain. The Spanish never could stop the incursions, and neither could their successors, the Mexicans. Though Mexico had a large standing army, the republic found itself too preoccupied with trying to put down rebellions to provide adequate protection to the people in scattered haciendas along and below the river. And in the early days of Texas settlement and annexation, the Comanches and other Indians took advantages of the strained relationship between the United States and Mexico to intensify their raiding south of the Rio Grande.

Picture the trail as two lengths of rope, frayed at the ends, crossing each other in a long, narrow X. A large spring marked the cross point. Big Spring, the seat of present Howard County, took its name from the oasis, which had attracted animal and man for millennia.

Young Comanches learned the geography of the trail from their elders, as they had learned it. The young men gathered in a circle and watched as an elder drew the route in the dirt and marked significant landmarks and water sources. The old warrior placed a stick with a single notch in the ground to indicate the location of the first camping place. Once satisfied that the novices understood the first day's route, he erased his drawing and outlined the second day's journey, using a stick with two notches to signify that day's stopping place. The Indians also may have used markings on buckskin as a crude map.

While exploring the Big Bend in 1849, U.S. Army captain Richard Whiting crossed the trail and later reported: "We struck a large Comanche warpath. Close together twenty-five deep-worn and much used trails made a great road, which told us that this was the highway by which each year the Comanches of the north desolate Durango and Chihuahua [Mexico]."

In 1852, using information gathered by U.S. Army captain Randolph B. Marcy and other explorers, J.H. Young compiled his *Map of the State of Texas from the Latest Authorities*. Published by Thomas Cowperwait and Company of Philadelphia, the map shows the Comanche War Trail with fair accuracy from Big Spring south to the Big Bend. On the map, an explanation adjacent to the Big Bend, where the lower crossing of the trail occurred, noted: "The Grand Indian Crossing is a shallow place in the Rio Grande 1,000 miles from its mouth, with 4 feet water. Here the…Comanches cross in their annual predatory incursions into Mexico."

Raiding along the trail continued unabated throughout Texas's near decade as an independent republic. Even for a few years after Texas's annexation to the United States, the annual raids went on. But in the early 1850s, the U.S. Army established forts at key points along the trail, including Fort Stockton at Comanche Springs. The army's main objective was to protect travelers headed west to California, but the location of these military posts at perennial Comanche water sources forced raiders to work harder to get to Mexico.

Eventually, as the frontier pushed farther west in Texas and the Comanches saw defeat in the Red River War of 1874–75 and relocated to a reservation in the Indian Territory (now Oklahoma), raiding along the trail ended.

The trail itself, like a scar from the vicious slash of a knife, remained visible for years. O.W. Williams, who came to west Texas in 1877 as a surveyor and settled in Fort Stockton, wrote that it was still clearly visible in the early 1900s: "Worn deep by the tracks of countless travelers—man and beast—and whitened by the bones of animals…it was a great chalk line on the map of West Texas from the Llano Estacado to the Rio Grande."

THE LEGEND OF INDIAN EMILY

One of the most romantic stories in the lore of the Old West originated at Fort Davis. The tale has been told and retold in all media. And now it's on the Internet. It's the story of Indian Emily and it goes like this.

In the late 1860s, an Apache female fell wounded in a skirmish between cavalry troops stationed at Fort Davis and her band. The soldiers took her back to the fort, where a woman named Mrs. Eason nursed her back to health and named her Emily. The Indian girl grew up on the post and eventually fell in love with Mrs. Eason's son, Lieutenant Tom Eason. But the soldier married a girl of his own culture and the brokenhearted Emily returned to her people.

Some time later, so the story continues, the Apaches planned a major assault on the fort. Emily, in an act of selfless love, slipped away from her village in the middle of the night to warn the young officer. As she approached the fort, a jittery sentry shot her. She died in Mrs. Eason's arms after proclaiming her everlasting love for Lieutenant Eason and warning of the impending attack on Fort Davis.

They buried Indian Emily at the post cemetery. After the army abandoned the garrison in 1891, the graves of most of the soldiers were relocated to the National Cemetery in San Antonio. Emily, however, was left behind.

The story goes back to 1919, when Carlysle Graham Raht included it in his book *Romance of the Davis Mountains and the Big Bend Country*. Raht said that the tale was confirmed by Henry O. Flipper, the first African American graduate of West Point and a one time lieutenant at Fort Davis. During the Texas centennial in 1936, the state placed a granite marker at Emily's grave. The inscription reduced her story to thirty-eight words, concluding that she had "saved the garrison from massacre."

Fort Davis at about the time an Apache woman supposedly saved the post from attack.

Alas, though touching, the account of Indian Emily and her valiant death is pure folklore. In 1969, as a reporter for the *San Angelo Standard-Times*, I had a hand in exposing it as such. I interviewed Franklin Smith, then superintendent of the Fort Davis National Historic Site, and asked him about the Indian Emily story.

"All evidence points against it," he said. In fact, he continued, National Park Service historians had refuted every aspect of the story. For one thing, Smith said, the National Archives had no record that a Lieutenant Tom Eason had ever been stationed at the fort. Further, researchers had found no record of a person by that name ever serving in the U.S. Army before 1903. And the park superintendent said that the military kept pretty good records, better than most people would think. Those records also showed that Fort Davis never experienced an attack by hostile Indians and that no assault had ever even been seriously anticipated.

Smith, who had done socioanthropological studies of the Apache culture, also said that Emily did not behave like an Apache woman in the story. "Her general behavior was, well...very un-Apache," he said. Though the legend has Emily being wounded during the fight with the soldiers, according to Smith, "Apache women didn't do any fighting except under dire circumstances."

Also, the circumstances of her supposed capture did not ring true. "Normally," Smith said, "when Indian dependents were captured, they were cared for as best as the Army could. They were usually farmed out to boarding schools. They were not normally kept around the forts."

Smith said that someone likely dreamed up the story after reading one too many Victorian romances. Sometime after my interview with him, the NPS removed the piled stones from Emily's purported grave, cut off access to the site and even took down the heavy historical marker, storing it along with other artifacts associated with the fort.

Fort Davis author Barry Scobee, one of the frequent tellers of the Indian Emily story, went to his own grave believing that it contained at least some elements of truth. He set forth two pieces of circumstantial evidence in his 1963 history of Fort Davis, *Fort Davis Texas 1583–1960*.

Scobee's Exhibit A came from a military report describing an engagement between three companies of Fort Davis troops under Lieutenant Patrick Cusack and a party of Indians on September 8, 1868. Following the fight, Cusack's command returned to the fort with two Mexican children who had been captured by the Indians, as well as "an Indian female child." Since local lore had Emily's death occurring in 1879 or '80, Scobee wrote, the child brought in by Cusack more than a decade earlier could have been her.

The writer offered as Exhibit B the recollection of David Merrill, the man who got the government contract to exhume the Fort Davis post cemetery. Merrill related that the military told him to dig up all the remains except for a soldier who had committed suicide and an Indian woman. He said that he removed eighty-nine sets of remains, though a later account has the number at eighty-three. No matter the count, he did not remove the Indian burial.

Scobee wrote that the grave had been marked by a board bearing an inscription that noted, "Indian Squaw—Died by Accident." By the time the state put up the historical marker, Scobee continued, the board had disappeared. Warren D. and Herbert D. Bloys, local old-timers, pointed out the grave's location and recalled the now politically incorrect wording of the wooden grave marker.

As Scobee wrote, "These bits of 'evidence'…constitute the supporting circumstances of Emily's reality." For a storyteller, killing off a legend is a mighty hard thing, almost as tough as putting down a good horse with a broken leg. Fortunately, a story does not have to be true to be engaging.

Soldiers

Zenas Bliss's High Country Scout

Good soldier that he was, Lieutenant Zenas Bliss reported to the colonel in command of Fort Davis that he had seen a stand of pine trees in the mountains not too far from the post.

Timber being a scarce commodity in the Big Bend, the colonel sent a detachment to see if wagons might be able to reach the spot. The soldiers rode to a point that Bliss estimated to be about eight miles from the pinery, as he called it, and made camp for the night.

After a light sunrise breakfast, Bliss, a sergeant and a scout set out on mules to ascend the mountains. "The mountains," Bliss later wrote in his memoir, "were so steep and fearfully difficult to travel over that we were much longer on the trail than I had anticipated, and did not get to the timber until after noon."

Realizing that he could not get back to camp the way he had come until after dark, Bliss figured that he could cross the mountain, strike the westward road to El Paso and circle back around. Having missed lunch, he hoped to be back to the main body of soldiers in time for a hot supper. But getting down the mountain proved almost as difficult as climbing it had been. "We were obliged to walk all the way, and lead our animals," he wrote.

They finally reached the road about sunset but were still a good twenty miles from camp and grub. And then their guide yelled, "Indians!" About three hundred yards off, Bliss made out three or four animals with what appeared to be packs on their backs. Indians could not be far away, he thought. The men dismounted, drew their rifles, took cover and settled down to see what would happen. The next time the figures came into view, Bliss and the others realized that they were antelope, not Apaches. "We had a good laugh at our mistake and went on our way to the El Paso road," he wrote.

That's when the bad weather hit. Dark and full of lightning, the thunderstorm forced the party to take shelter in a live oak grove. Even so, Bliss's buckskin trousers soon were "as wet as a sponge full of water."

The rain stopped, but then the wind picked up from the north. Still miles from camp, Bliss ordered a stop for the night. With no overcoats or blankets—and wet matches—the soldiers spent a miserable night shivering in the cold.

"My buckskin pants were frozen stiff in the morning," Bliss wrote, "and before mounting we all ran up and down the road to limber up and thaw ourselves out." Their guide said that he had been colder before but had never spent the night under a buzzard roost. Insult having been added to injury, he woke up covered in bird droppings.

Bliss and the other two men made it back to camp by noon. "We were thoroughly fatigued," he understated. "We had been about thirty hours

As a young officer, Zenas Bliss had a rough scout in the Big Bend.

without anything to eat, and had hardly slept a wink all night, and had ridden a good many hours, even though we had not covered many miles."

Despite their exertion, though they had been able to more accurately fix the location of the timber, they hadn't found a passable trail. A road was later cut to the area, and the wood was used for improvements at the fort, saving taxpayers the expense of shipping lumber in from elsewhere.

Bliss's mountain scout began on April 17, 1855—his twenty-second birthday. "It was a cold day for a birthday ride," he concluded.

Camp Pena Colorado Outlasted Fort Davis

On a blazing August day in 1879, two companies of the Twenty-fifth Infantry halted beneath a high red bluff four miles southwest of present Marathon. Though far from the first men to stop at the springs that bubbled below the massive rocks, the blue-coated soldiers would be the first to stay for an extended period.

The water hole was a landmark on the Comanche Trail, the wide, well-worn route raiding war parties took each fall from the South Plains deep into Mexico. From the springs, the trail ran south into the Big Bend, where it forked before crossing the Rio Grande. The military had known of the water hole for at least twenty years. In July 1859, a camel-mounted expedition under Lieutenant William H. Echols had stopped there to water their strange mounts.

The exact date troops arrived at Pena Colorado is not known, but companies F and G of the Twenty-fifth Infantry had been ordered on August 13, 1879, to march southwest from Fort Stockton "without delay" to the spring to establish the new camp. The orders came from Colonel Benjamin H. Grierson, the Civil War veteran who commanded the military's District of the Pecos from his headquarters at Fort Concho at San Angelo.

The troopers who established the new camp may have been seasoned soldiers but were certainly not carpenters. Nevertheless, they did the best they could with what they had. "We had no tools for that sort of work," Nato Payne, a Seminole Indian scout, later told his grandson, Blas Payne. "The rocks for the walls were gathered from off the points of nearby mountains and put together with our fingers, by using mud."

Frequent flooding of the nearby creek forced the military to relocate the camp half a mile from its original site. A proofreading error moved the

Army camels came through the future location of Camp Pena Colorado in 1859.

camp even farther, at least on paper. Somewhere along the line, a comma got inserted between "Pena" and "Colorado," giving the impression that the post guarded some point in or near the Rocky Mountains rather than the Texas portion of the Chihuahuan Desert.

Never formally planned, the post grew sporadically. Consequently, most soldiers did not view being stationed at Camp Pena Colorado as a plum assignment. "It is very disheartening to the officers to be compelled, through the cold winters and hot summers of West Texas, to keep their wives and children in tents, shanties, or brush huts," Grierson reported a few months after the camp's establishment.

With the completion of the first rail line across the Trans-Pecos in 1881, the military in the Big Bend had an easier time getting supplies, but four years later, Camp Pena Colorado had seen no improvement in living conditions. "The roofs of the officer's and men's quarters are of brush and dirt covered with canvas and all leak," a quartermaster's report noted in 1885. "They are ill-conceived and most involve continual expense to keep in habitable order…Some of the buildings are not worth further labor in repairs."

The camp did have a couple of things going for it. For one, the spring fed a fine swimming hole. Floating in metal washtubs, troopers kept cool and had fun at the same time by playing water polo or staging "boat" races. Also, the scenery was nice and the hunting good. "Antelopes could be seen at anytime of the day from a low hill a mile from our little huts," one officer stationed there wrote. Accordingly, fresh antelope meat added variety to the soldiers' chow.

In another plus, at least from the standpoint of the officers, the camp lay thirty miles from the nearest town—in other words, it was a full day's ride to the closest place to get a drink, gamble or consort with bawds. "The habits of the [enlisted] men are very good," Lieutenant George K. Hunter reported, noting that this mainly could be attributed to the distance from temptation. That, he concluded, "relieves the soldier from demoralizing influence."

Since July 1884, the post had been garrisoned by troopers of the Tenth Cavalry, including Lieutenant Henry O. Flipper, the first black to graduate from West Point. When the military transferred elements of the Tenth

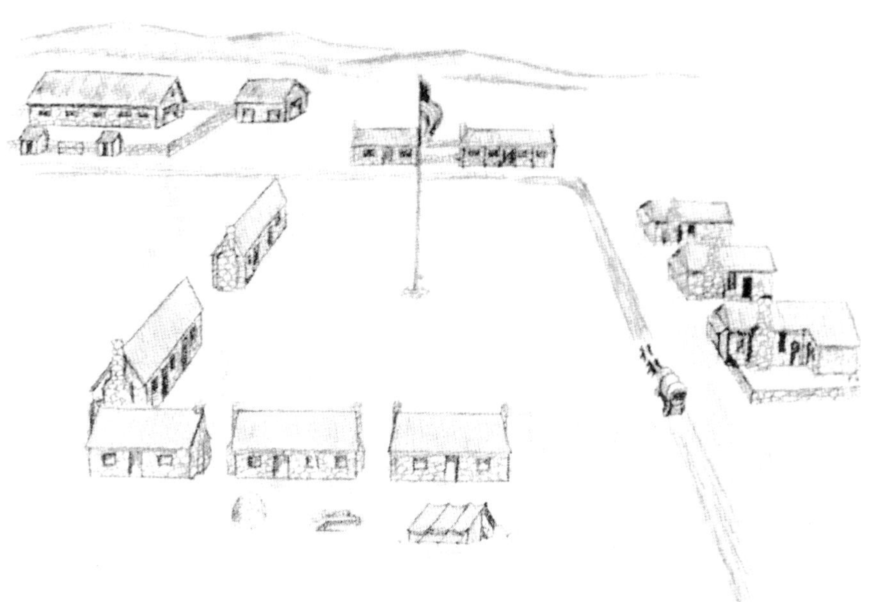

Camp Pena Colorado came after Fort Davis, but it lasted longer.

Cavalry to Arizona to try to find Geronimo and his hostile band of Apaches, a contingent from the Third Cavalry took over the post.

A report compiled in 1886 lists the camp buildings. One of the three officers' quarters was made of stone and plastered with mud. The author of the report adjudged the building's overall condition as merely fair, with the other two officers' quarters of adobe with canvas roofs described as "very poor." The post surgeon occupied a brush-and-mud structure with a rough board floor but no ceiling. The camp's other buildings included a headquarters of stone and mud roofed with a tarp, two barracks, a quartermaster's office, a guardhouse and a storehouse.

As the 1880s came to a close, hostile Indians no longer posed a threat to Texas. The army began to make plans to abandon its longtime garrison at Fort Davis, but since Camp Pena Colorado lay closer to the transcontinental railroad, the brass at the San Antonio headquarters of the Department of Texas considered making it a permanent post to watch over the Big Bend. That's why when the last soldier marched out of Fort Davis in 1891, the U.S. flag still flew over Pena Colorado. But not for long. The military changed its mind, and in December 1892 the last unit stationed at the camp, Troop E, Third Cavalry, got orders to vacate the post. By January 30, 1893, the camp had been deserted.

Camp Pena Colorado never acquired the mystique attached over the years to the larger Fort Davis, but as an active military post, it outlasted it more than a year.

"That Added Zest of Danger"

Colonel James J. Hornbrook had been trained by the military to fight, not write, but the veteran cavalry officer proved to be no raw recruit when it came to marshaling words. But enlisting men was what he had in mind when he published a notice seeking men interested in signing up for a hitch in the Fifth U.S. Cavalry, which then had a significant presence in the Big Bend.

"Does the idea of patrolling this historic and history making country where every man is on his own make your pulse beat a bit faster?" he asked. "Wouldn't you like to be in one of the wildest, least explored sections and the only real frontier of the greatest nation on earth?"

The colonel touted the area's "rugged mountains, deep canyons, [and] rocky precipices," the area's abundance of huntable wildlife and the fact

The army sought men looking for adventure to serve along the Texas border.

that it lay one hundred miles from the railroad. "Join the Fifth Cavalry if you are for really honest-to-God outdoor life and next to nature stuff," the colonel waxed on. "We have it and are enjoying every minute of it, and we are calling to any man—and that is every man—whose heart and soul yearns for the riches we have, and who hasn't the necessary riches to enjoy them."

He concluded: "The Fifth Cavalry wants real men: men who like to rough it. We need you and you need us and our wonderful Big Bend District with all its vastness, all its wildness, and that added zest of danger that all men desire. Sign up now while the spirit moves."

Not only was the army trying to encourage enlistment for service as a horse soldier in the Big Bend, work also continued to make those soldiers more comfortable in a land that could be unforgiving. Though the transition to gasoline-powered motor vehicles had begun, the army still depended on soldiers on horseback, supplied by pack mules or mule-pulled wagons during the border buildup following the outbreak of the Mexican Revolution. Because of the long distances involved, and the fact that cavalry could only move thirty to forty miles a day, the military had established a series of outposts up and down the border.

"Twice a day every foot of the borderline is patrolled by cavalrymen and infantrymen, while the complete circuit of the various stations is made always once and sometimes twice or thrice a day by airmen," the *New York Times* reported on January 25, 1920.

For nearly two decades, soldiers stationed at remote points in the Big Bend made do—as a quasi-official organ called the *Quartermaster Review* reported in 1925—"with only tents and shacks for shelter, hauling their own water from the Rio Grande and enduring...intense heat and bitter cold."

Finally, someone in the War Department had an idea that the troops in the field must have applauded. The military decided to spend $8.5 million for labor and material to build modern facilities at forty-nine stations along the Rio Grande.

Eleven of those outposts would be along or near the Rio Grande south of Marfa, the military headquarters for the Big Bend, "radiating like the spokes of a wheel, with Marfa as a center, averaging some 170 miles across high mountains and over trails that were hard on pack trains."

Because of the difficulty of transporting building material over such rough terrain and over such long distances, the army had an even better idea: use sun-dried adobe made by mixing straw with clay from the banks of the Rio Grande. "These adobe buildings have the characteristic of being far cooler in summer and very much warmer in winter than wooden buildings," the

During the Mexican Revolution, the army had camps scattered all across the Big Bend.

article noted. In addition, adobe structures could not burn and tended to last a long time.

The idea must have originated in Texas, where savvy officers understood the local culture. As the article in the *Review* put it, "A proposal was made to the War Department to build adobe barracks of a special design, utilizing the old ideas which had been in use in Mexico since the time of the Aztec Indians and some modern ideas to meet the old defects."

The modern idea involved reinforcing the foot-thick adobe with heavy wire mesh, covered with hard finish plaster to protect the water-soluble brick from weather (in the odd event that it ever rained in that country). In addition to the adobe barracks, officers' quarters, mess halls and lavatories, all of the outposts had water, sewage and electricity furnished by World War I surplus generators.

Though the use of adobe proved effective and doubtless saved some tax dollars, the construction project proved to be too much, too late. No sooner had all the improvements been made than the turmoil in Mexico quieted and peacefulness descended on the border.

How successful Colonel Hornbrook's rosy prose aimed at attracting young men to the Big Bend turned out to have been is not known, but about the time all of the new construction had been completed, the army abandoned most of the outposts in the area. Even so, the adobe installations served as periodic bivouacs during training maneuvers and routine patrols for as long as the military guarded the border with horse soldiers, an effort that continued through the beginning of World War II.

Critters

The Davis Mountain Grizzly

If he were still alive, Joe M. Evans would be pleased that the black bear has reestablished itself in the high country of Texas. Of course, Evans and other sport hunters had a fair amount to do with the virtual disappearance of the black bear from its historic habitat in the Davis Mountains of far west Texas and elsewhere in the Big Bend.

In January 1903, Texas land commissioner J.J. Terrell spent a couple of weeks bear hunting in the Davis Mountains. He and his party took six bears. When he returned to Austin, Terrell sent President Theodore Roosevelt an invitation to join him on his next hunt.

Roosevelt was not able to work a trip to the Big Bend into his schedule, but in November Terrell and his two brothers, J.P. Terrell of Temple and C.V. Terrell of Decatur, returned to the Davis Mountains for a week of hunting with Joe Evans's father, George, and his uncle, John Z. Means, serving as guides and furnishing dogs. The hunting party saw fifteen bears and killed five.

J.P. Terrell photographed one bear treed by a dog and then brought it tumbling down with a .30-.30 slug in its heart, reported the *Galveston Daily News* on November 23 that year. "During the several years I have been in Austin this is the greatest recreation I've taken," said the land commissioner of his high country trip. Terrell said that he had hunted buffalo on the plains as a young man but that "shooting buffalo was not half such a sport as

BEAR STORIES

By

JOE M. EVANS

Del Norte Hotel El Paso, Texas

PRICE $1.00

The cover of the booklet that Joe Evans wrote about bear hunting in the Davis Mountains.

chasing bears." His brother J.P. agreed: "I had the best time of all my life; we had a jolly crowd, good music, plenty to eat and unfailing appetites."

Occasionally, a bear in the Davis Mountain came close to reversing the roles of hunter and hunted. In the fall of 1913, Wood Mendel of Alpine shot a bear cub that he found in a cave. As he began dragging out its carcass, the cub's enraged mama showed up and charged. He shot her and then unwisely put down his rifle to haul her from the cave's entrance. Preoccupied with that task, he noticed too late the arrival of a third bear. The bear attacked, biting and clawing. Mendel finally killed the bear by choking it. At least, that's what he claimed. However he subdued the bear, he lived to tell the tale.

Years later, Joe Evans wrote and published a pamphlet called *Bear Stories*. In a Sacramento used bookshop some years back, casually pawing through a box like a mildly hungry bear checking out a picnic basket, I found a copy. It sold for only a dollar when published, but now it's a scarce piece of Texana, and I brought it back from California to the Lone Star state, where it belongs.

The best tale in the booklet is about the only grizzly bear ever documented in the Davis Mountains. In fact, the grizzly was the only one ever known to have been killed anywhere in Texas. To appreciate the significance of that, it's important to understand the difference between a black bear and a grizzly bear. Black bears are content eating berries and nuts. Grizzlies are carnivores. Not named *Ursus horribilis* for nothing, they will happily attack and eat livestock or humans. When standing on their hind legs, an adult male can tower up to seven or eight feet.

Evans and others who hunted black bear in the Davis Mountains during the late nineteenth century and the first few decades of the twentieth century saw it as a grand adventure. Today, conservationists realize that overhunting nearly exterminated the bear in Texas. But the killing of the bear Evans called "the Big Grizzly" was probably the end of the line for a unique grizzly species labeled *texensis*.

"We had an annual bear hunt in the Davis Mountains…where we took our family," Evans wrote. "On some hunts we would kill as many as ten bear, a mountain lion or two and possibly a lobo wolf and the trees around camp were hanging full of deer and antelope. Those were happy days."

Texas's only grizzly bear came out of aptly named Saw Tooth Mountain in Jeff Davis County.

Out after black bear on November 2, 1890, they rode up on a dead, partially eaten cow in a gulch near the head of Limpia Creek in Jeff Davis County. Not far from the carcass, the hunters noticed a bed of pine needles ten feet long. Close to the lair lay a final, unmistakable clue: a bear track thirteen inches long and nearly six inches across. The hunters knew that they had found the handiwork of a grizzly.

The giant bear had dragged the cow for one hundred yards down the side of a mountain. "In doing so," former Texas Ranger A.J. Sowell related in an article he later wrote for a San Antonio newspaper, "[the grizzly] hung her around a small tree, but…continued to pull until he broke the tree down and then went on with his load, breaking the horns off the cow when they would hang on rocks."

Of thirty-five dogs the hunters had, only four had the tenacity—or lack of intelligence—to take up the grizzly's trail. Their noses to the ground, the dogs followed the big animal's scent for five miles, finally cornering him in a stand of pine trees.

The first two hunters to reach the standoff, John Means and C.O. Finley, cut loose on the grizzly. Each man put five rifle slugs in the bear, which they later estimated weighed 1,000 pounds. Another source said that the bear actually weighed 1,100 hundred pounds, and still another account had the bear at 1,200 pounds. No matter where it tipped the scales, it was a huge animal.

From a mile away, the other hunters could hear the wounded bear bellowing like a bull, the great male's death cries reverberating off the ancient igneous rock piled along the canyon. Before he died, the grizzly killed one of the four dogs with a powerful swing of one of his huge paws. "He literally broke the dog to pieces," Evans wrote.

The hunters had the bear's skin—which took four men to load onto a packhorse—tanned and mounted. Even after its head and legs had been removed, the hide could cover a double bed. The bear's skull ended up in the Smithsonian Institution in Washington. In 1918, a scientist assigned subspecies status to the animal to which it had once belonged. During the Texas centennial in 1935–36, Evans enlisted the help of his congressman to get the skull loaned for a time for display in Texas, but the staff of the Washington, D.C., museum said that they considered the specimen too rare to be displayed outside the museum.

Today, the Texas Parks and Wildlife Department says that black bears have reestablished themselves in the Big Bend, but no one has seen a grizzly or any sure sign of one in the Lone Star state since Victorian times. In 1931, someone found tracks that may have been made by another grizzly in the Guadalupe Mountains, but no one ever saw the bear.

If Evans felt any twinge of regret over having had a hand in the demise of the only grizzly ever known to have trod Texas, he did not betray that in his booklet: "The killing of this grizzly was the climax [of] all our hunting experiences in the Davis Mountains."

Taps for Louie

The buglers sounded "Adjutant's Call," and a squadron of tan-clad cavalry troopers moved forward at a trot. That cold winter morning, December 14, 1932, was a sad one for old-time horse soldiers and civilians alike at Fort D.A. Russell in Marfa—they both realized that they were witnessing the end of an era.

Troops rode from their stables to the parade ground at about 9:30 a.m. The cavalrymen passed the reviewing stand at a slow walk, sabers raised as each platoon passed Colonel William A. Austin and his staff. Red-and-white guidons dipped in the customary "Hail and Farewell" salute. The regiment turned at a faster gait and reassembled facing the review stand. After a brief honors ceremony, the colonel addressed the men.

Following Austin's talk, every officer and enlisted man in the regiment dismounted and turned to face his horse. The men stood for a long moment with hands on the polls of their mounts in a silent farewell. Then a trooper led a lone horse, caparisoned in black, to the front of the regiment. The horse was Louie, the oldest mount in the historic First Cavalry, the regiment then stationed at the remote Big Bend post.

At the bugle call of "Boots and Saddles," the six hundred men of the command mounted their horses for the last time. The regiment would soon be transferred to Fort Knox, Kentucky, where it would be merged with another unit to become a mechanized outfit. Taps was sounded, the lines broke and the troopers returned individually to their stables with their horses.

Louie, a cavalry mount since shortly after the turn of the century, had served in the tropics, during the Mexican border troubles and during World War I. Now he stood tied to the reviewing stand. The regiment, now afoot, marched past, their sabers drawn in salute to their comrade.

The other horses of the regiment would be shipped to other border posts, but not Louie. The thirty-four-year-old horse—roughly equivalent to ninety-

THE BARRACKS BAG

VOLUME I — FORT D. A. RUSSELL, TEXAS, FEBRUARY 18, 1942 — NUMBER 16

"Old Louie," Reminder Of Famed Black Hawks Adds His Name To History of Fort D. A. Russell

You could leave Post Headquarters at Fort D. A. Russell this afternoon and go across to the Post Gymnasium. There you could take the road that leads down through the reservation just back of the main line of Barracks. If you followed that road two-thirds of the way down the line, you might notice a sort of stone monument with the Black Hawk insignia of the First Cavalry—now armored. You read the inscription, 'Animo et Fide," meaning "Friend and Faithful." You might even notice the shape of the rock border without realizing that it was a grave—Louie's grave.

As poignant and as colorful as life itself is the story of Louie. His service record would have been the envy of the Army's best Master Sergeant and his experiences would have made Motion Picture History. He had served the First Cavalry faithfully for a period of twenty-eight years through tropics and cold, through rain and sand, through war and peace.

Louie was buried in the Troop B area December 11, 1932, just before the First Cavalry was moved from this Post to Fort Knox. The orders

Picture by Keith Stone

faster gaits and following the review it was reassembled facing the reviewing stand.

The enlisted men entitled to become Knights of the Black Hawk were about to be inducted into that organization. These men had served in the First Cavalry at least one en-

the stables. The Standard Bearers dismounted and bore the colors from the field.

After the troops had returned to their stables, their led horses were left at the Troop picket lines and all mounted men returned to the parade ground where mounted saber charges

Fort Bliss' Ire Is Up As Infantry Tries to Take Girl

Pretty Mary Ann Mercer "Huddle Girl" for Cavalry But Ga. Infantry Gets Ideas

The First Cavalry Division at Fort Bliss is buying Defense Bonds and Stamps like their very life depended upon it. Artillery Units are now leading in the race with a staggering $15,614.55 and the Eighth Cavalry is runner-up with $10,854.65 to their credit.

And the whole thing started over that little Mercer girl, you know the one. She sings on Uncle Walter's Dog House Show. The First Infantry training Regiment at Camp Wheeler, Ga., got to scheming how they would make this pretty thing their "One and Only." The Cavalry had different ideas. Now the "war" is on.

This Twentieth Century civil war started when the First Infantry boys fell victim en masse to Mary Ann's charms, chose her as their "Favorite Date" and invited her to appear at their Valentine Party on February 14.

A post newspaper at Marfa's Fort D.A. Russell covered the "retirement" of Louie.

nine in human years—would be put down. At sundown, with his escort moving to the slow beat of the "Death March," Louie slowly walked to his final resting place. With a ceremonial volley of shots and the sad notes of taps, a squad buried the First Cavalry's oldest horse. A gray stone bearing the regiment's famed Black Hawk insignia eventually marked his grave.

The post at Marfa, established in 1911 and home of the First Cavalry since 1923, continued in operation through World War II. The army abandoned the fort in 1949 and sold the buildings and the land. But Louie's grave remained in the once wild country he had helped to protect.

Drawing the Map

In the Beginning, There Was Bexar

In the beginning, there was Bexar. Well, the heavens and earth came first, but in Texas history, Bexar County is about as fundamental as it gets considering land ownership.

Dating back to the late Mexican period, for administrative purposes the province of Texas consisted of four departments. One of those departments was Bexar, with San Antonio its only settlement. The Department of Bexar stretched from the Nueces River in the south to the Red River in the north, but it would get bigger.

After Texas won its independence from Mexico in 1836, the Congress of the Republic of Texas started organizing the new nation. Late in its first year of existence, the Texas Congress designated twenty-three counties. One of those original counties was Bexar, large enough to have been its own state or country.

The original Bexar County took in even more real estate than the old Department of Bexar. It now extended beyond the Pecos as far west as El Paso, as far south as the Rio Grande Valley and as far north as what is now the top of the Panhandle. On the east it was roughly bounded by an imaginary north–south line bisecting the state's center.

When Texas became the twenty-eighth state in the Union in 1845, the first state legislature transformed Bexar County into the Bexar Land District. Not that it had many people, but the district still included roughly half of the Texas we know today.

As Texas grew slowly to the west, the district slowly shrunk as the legislature created new counties. In 1846, the Bexar Land District lost the valley, as everything south of the Nueces River became Nueces County. When Bandera County came into being in 1856, the Bexar Land District existed for the first time as a separate entity from Bexar County. Even so, the district still covered about a quarter of the state.

The Trans-Pecos and Big Bend remained part of the sprawling Bexar Land District until 1850. That year, the legislature created El Paso and Presidio Counties. But another two decades went by before either county was actually organized. (Presidio County saw partial organization in 1858, with Presidio del Norte, now simply Presidio, as county seat.)

El Paso County was organized on March 7, 1871, with San Elizario as county seat. Full organization for Presidio County finally came in 1875, when Fort Davis was named the county's capital. Four years after the railroad passed through in 1881, the new town of Marfa took over as county seat.

Presidio County stood as is until 1871, when the legislature sliced off its northwestern third, creating Pecos County, a political subdivision that stretched from the New Mexico border on the northwest to the Rio Grande on the southwest. Fort Stockton became the county seat with the county's organization on June 13, 1872. Pecos County lost its northwest third in 1883 with the creation of Reeves County, with Pecos City as county seat.

Still a giant, Presidio County got sliced into five counties in 1887, with the creation of Brewster, Buchel, Foley and Jeff Davis Counties. (See the next section for more detail on these counties.)

The next change to the map of the Big Bend came via legislative fiat on April 8, 1905, with the creation of Terrell County, which previously had been the bottom third of Pecos County. The new county was named for Alexander Watkins Terrell, a southerner who had the good sense to come to the Lone Star state in 1852.

After fighting in the Civil War, he settled in Houston to practice law. But, as an early biography put it, "owing to the unsettled condition of the courts" (in Harris County), he moved to a plantation on the Brazos River in Robertson County. After four years as a gentleman farmer, he moved to Austin in 1872.

Three years after becoming a resident of the capital city, Terrell won election to the state senate. After seven years in the upper chamber, the "urgent solicitation of his fellow citizens" resulted in his running for a seat in the House. In all, he served sixteen years in the legislature, earning a reputation as having been "the author of more good laws for Texas than any other man, living or dead." Speaking of the dead, unlike the namesakes of most Texas counties, Terrell lived to see a county named in his honor. He died on September 9, 1912, and is buried in Austin.

El Paso County took the next hit in 1911, losing its eastern end with the creation of Culberson County. The new county honored Texas congressman David B. Culberson and became the fourth largest in the state.

The final Trans-Pecos baby Bexar—though as Texas's second-largest county it's hardly a baby in size—was Hudspeth County. Also cut from El Paso County, the new county was organized in February 1917. Like Culberson County, Hudspeth County honored a U.S. House member, Congressman Claude Benton Hudspeth.

Today Texas has 254 political subdivisions known as counties—and 128 of them, including all of the counties encompassing the Big Bend, once were part of Bexar County. It's hard to tell without running a survey, but a casual examination of a map showing the evolution of the state's counties indicates at least another dozen or so counties that had been partially located in the original Bexar County. Thanks to generations of legislative whittling, the original Bexar County is now a mere slip of itself, only 1,248 square miles. But it's the granddaddy of half of Texas and all of the Big Bend.

Alpine Courthouse Once Served Three Counties

As Texas courthouses go, the 1888 two-story building in Alpine that accommodates the government officials of Brewster County isn't all that impressive. The state has older courthouses, it has more architecturally interesting courthouses and it has bigger courthouses. But of Texas's 254 county capitols, only one of them has ever served three different counties. And that would be the Brewster County Courthouse.

The story begins more than four hundred miles east of the Big Bend in Austin, where in the spring of 1887 the Texas legislature broke giant Presidio County into five different counties. With the coming of the railroad in 1881, the area had grown in population. But while railroads made transportation across Texas easier and faster, the horse remained the primary mode of travel. So that no one would have to ride more than thirty miles to the nearest courthouse, lawmakers for years had slowly been chopping up large counties into smaller ones.

Brewster County Courthouse in Alpine. *Courtesy Alpine Chamber of Commerce.*

The new counties carved from Presidio would be Buchel, Brewster, Foley and Jeff Davis. Marfa would continue as county seat of what remained of Presidio County, Fort Davis would be the capital of Jeff Davis County and Murpheyville (soon to become Alpine) would be the seat of Brewster County. The town also would serve as the county seat of Buchel and Foley Counties until they could be organized.

Lawmakers named Brewster County after Henry Percy Brewster, who happened to arrive in Texas from South Carolina on March 2, 1836—the day Texas declared its independence from Mexico. He took part in the Battle of San Jacinto and quickly rose to the position of secretary of war after the government of the Republic of Texas was organized under President David G. Burnet. After reading the law, he gained admission to the bar in 1837. Brewster served as a district attorney and, after Texas became the twenty-eighth state of the Union, he held the office of attorney general under Governor George T. Wood. In 1855, he left Texas for a time to practice international law in Washington, D.C., but he came back to the South to join the Confederate army when the Civil War broke out. Back in Texas after the war, he settled in San Antonio, where he again practiced law. Governor John Ireland named him commissioner of insurance, statistics and history on January 29, 1883. He still held that office when he died three days after Christmas in 1884. He had a long and distinguished career, but one thing he didn't do was ever set foot in the part of Texas that would be named in his honor.

While Jeff Davis County commemorated the former Confederate president, Jefferson Finis Davis, Foley County was different—it actually honored three people: the brothers Arthur, James and Tucker Foley. All of them died violently in early Texas. Arthur Foley was executed with Colonel

James Fannin's men at Goliad in 1836, James Foley was killed by Mexicans in 1839 near the Nueces River and Tucker Foley was killed by Comanches in 1840 in Lavaca County.

Like Brewster, Foley and Jeff Davis Counties, Buchel County commemorated the name of a man who never saw the Big Bend: Augustus C. Buchel, a German who immigrated to Texas in 1845, settling at the port town of Indianola. He fought in the Mexican-American War and the Civil War, dying in the Battle of Pleasant Hill in Louisiana on April 9, 1864.

Surviving records do not reflect the name of the architect who designed the Brewster County Courthouse, but whoever drew the plans for the building did not waste any time with innovation. Instead, he provided specifications for a traditional structure of the French Second Empire style. (Similar courthouses stood in Caldwell, Concho, Goliad, Hill, Hood, Lampasas, Parker and Shackelford Counties.)

The contractor who built the Alpine courthouse was Tom Lovell, a builder who had constructed five other courthouses elsewhere in the state. For Brewster County's "temple of justice," he used dark red bricks from kilns in nearby Ranger Canyon. The building stands on a limestone base.

For a decade, the handful of residents living in Buchel and Foley Counties came to the new courthouse in Alpine to pay their taxes, file a deed or a lawsuit, sit on a jury, see the sheriff or do anything else involving county government.

One of the lawyers who did business in the Brewster County Courthouse was Wigfall Van Sickle. Born in east Texas in 1863, he came to Alpine in 1885 to teach school. While educating youngsters, though, he continued to learn on his own, reading the law and gaining admission to the bar. In 1888, he successfully ran for county judge.

Van Sickle had actively lobbied the legislature for the creation of Brewster County, but by 1897 he saw no need for Buchel and Foley Counties. If either were to be organized, their county seats would grow and siphon business from Alpine. So the judge took the train to Austin and succeeded in getting the legislature to pass a bill abolishing the two unorganized political subdivisions on the eastern flank of Brewster County. Two years later, residents of that half of Brewster County tried to get the legislature to reconstitute the two counties, but lawmakers weren't interested.

Today, Buchel and Foley Counties exist only on old maps, even though they honor some deserving early Texans.

\

Ghost Towns

Lindsey City

Lindsey City is such an ethereal ghost town that it doesn't even show up on the list of Texas ghost towns. But it existed, and as was the case with just about every ghost town, its residents once figured that their city had an unlimited future.

"Lindsey City is growing in proportion to the city of Boquillas on the other side of the Rio Grande City," a correspondent who called himself "Kodak" wrote to the *Eagle Pass Guide*, a newspaper published downstream from the Big Bend in Maverick County. "Favorable reports continue to come from the mines and the Mexican government will soon commence work on a wagon road from the mines to Cuartro Ciengas."

Kodak wrote that report in May 1896, a couple of years after D.E. Lindsey had established a trading post on the Texas side of the river, across from Boquillas, Mexico. Because of the mining activity in Mexico on the part of the Kansas City Smelting Company, business at the store was good. But Lindsey and Kodak both realized that with improved transportation the picture could be even brighter. For hundreds of mine workers, the Lindsey store was the closest place to buy American products.

A man named Frank Ashton had been surveying a wagon road from the mines in Mexico that would cross the river and proceed to Marathon, the closest connection to the Southern Pacific Railroad. "Should the company decide on a road it surely must follow that a port will be established here, and Lindsey City will soon assume some proportions," Kodak reflected.

The other big news in Lindsey City that Gay Nineties spring was matrimonial. Kodak went on to report the wedding of one of Lindsey's clerks to a senorita from Boquillas, an event witnessed "by a large company of the leading citizens." The day after the wedding came Cinco de Mayo, the holiday in observance of Benito Juárez' decisive defeat of the French in 1867. People from both sides of the river enjoyed a parade and speeches, Kodak reported. "Among the amusements was a phonograph exhibition by Mr. Tom W. Peake, of this city," the writer continued. "Mr. Stanley Peake arrived just in time from Marathon with a number of new records of Spanish national music, ordered specially from New York. 'Certamen Nacional' and 'Las Golondrinas' were well received."

A party couldn't go on forever, and neither did Lindsey City. It turned out that another wedding killed the town. While attending a *baille* (dance) in Mexico, Lindsey became acquainted with the most attractive young lady he had ever had the pleasure of seeing. In dancing away one night, Lindsey started thinking in terms of always and forever. As area historian Hallie Stillwell later wrote, "When love strikes in the Big Bend, it strikes like lightning."

The store owner soon sent a note to the woman's father, asking his permission to marry her. The father said yes, and another wedding was on. But Lindsey's partner, Charlie Hess, was a confirmed bachelor. He didn't like the idea of having a woman around and soon sold his interest in the business to Lindsey. The Lindseys stayed in the area for a while but eventually moved to San Antonio to raise a family.

There's still a small store on the Texas side across from Boquillas catering to Big Bend National Park visitors and residents of Mexico. But the mines that once gave the area hope of prosperity are long abandoned, and no one living remembers the glory days of Lindsey City, a town arguably killed by love.

Tesnus

Tesnus is a stealthy ghost town—except for a railroad siding and a sign, no physical evidence of it remains.

Founded in 1882 when the tracks of the Southern Pacific Railroad reached a point twenty-three miles southeast of Marathon in sprawling Brewster

County, the town (a stretch of the word) consisted of a railroad section house, houses for the section foreman and the water pumper, a telegrapher's house and a few other structures. In addition to its role in keeping the tracks maintained and the locomotive boilers full, Tesnus provided ranchers a way to ship their cattle to market.

First called Tabor, the railroad enclave lost that name when a post office application got rejected by Washington because a similarly named town already existed in Brazos County. Then Sunset arose as a fitting name for the place, considering that the famed Sunset Limited passenger train came through each day. But Montague County had a monopoly on Sunset, Texas. Someone finally came up with a solution to the name problem that met the approval of the U.S. Postal Service, but more of that in a bit.

In 1945, the railroad installed a new man as signal maintainer at Tesnus. He arrived with his wife, who became the Tesnus postmistress, and five of their seven kids. (Two of their girls had married and lived elsewhere.)

The addition of this new family pushed Tesnus's population up to about twenty people. Throw in the folks who lived on the surrounding ranch, and the postmistress had a small but consistent volume of mail to handle.

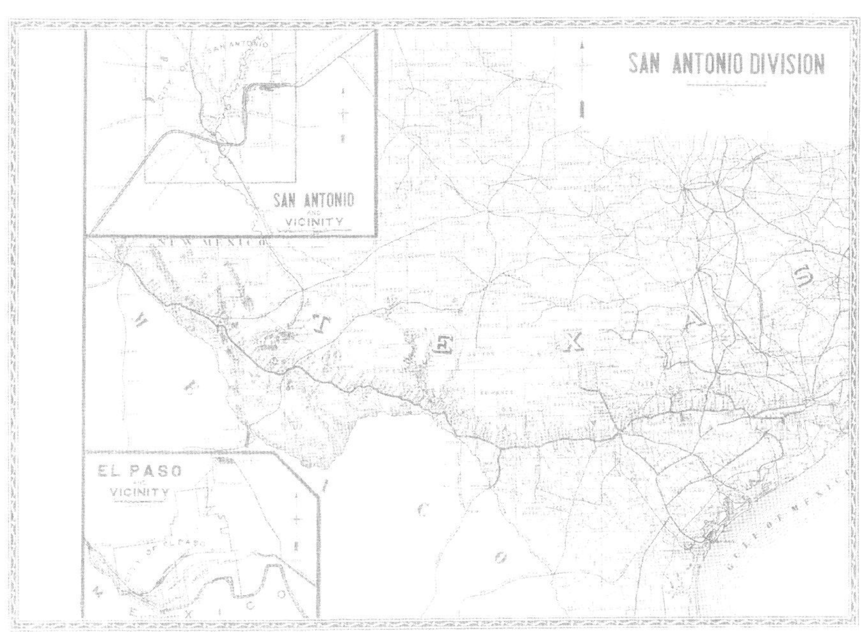

Southern Pacific map showing Tesnus and other Big Bend towns.

"Patrons came up the steps to the front porch, and she served [them] through her bedroom window," remembers one of the signal maintainer's children, who because of the career she had as a caseworker for a state protective agency asked not to be identified. "Maxon and Haymond were the railroad towns on either side of Tesnus, and those who lived in them and a ranch foreman came to Tesnus to get their mail," she recalled.

Occasionally, the railroad would move in a work crew that lived in temporary housing that the company had constructed. At other times, workers would stay in gang cars left on the siding for weeks or months until a particular maintenance project got completed.

Despite the occasional influx of additional railroad workers, not much ever happened in Tesnus. The most sensational crime was when the assistant telegraph operator went on a toot and shot up the Tesnus sign. Occasionally, a railroad bull (detective) or train crewman would throw a hobo off a train, leaving him temporarily stranded there. "Mama would feed them in return for chopping kindling," the former resident said.

One time a skunk got into the chicken coop. "I was supposed to hold the dog while Mama shot the skunk," she said. "But he was bigger than I was and broke away. Got there about the time Mama shot, but the skunk sprayed her, my sister and the dog. Tomato juice helps, but nothing cures except time."

When a train hit a deer and word reached town in time for the meat to still be fresh, her brothers hurried to the spot, field-dressed it and cut it up

The signal maintainer's house in long-vanished Tesnus during the 1940s after a snowfall.

for venison for the family table. Classic big brothers, they once barbecued a rattlesnake steak and tried to talk their little sister into eating it. While she didn't fall for that, the brothers did serve her older sister grilled mockingbird one time, telling her that it was dove.

Of Tesnus, she continued: "It was mostly a railroad town, in the middle of the Gage Ranch. There was a siding for trains to meet or pass one another, and it was a place for the chugga puffers [steam locomotives] to stop for water, coal and salt. (There was ice in the refrigerator cars.)" She said that the ranch foreman lived in a house on the dirt road to Marathon, inside of a mile from Tesnus.

So how did they finally come up with a lasting name for Tabor cum Sunset? Proving once again the power of simplicity, to use railroad metaphor, someone suggested switching the caboose with the locomotive and spelling Sunset backward, as in T-e-s-n-u-s.

But clever nomenclature is powerless against change. With diesel-powered trains needing fewer stops than "chugga puffers," the railroad closed its operations in Tesnus midway into the 1950s. When word got out that Tesnus would be no more, the town's last postmistress had one last flurry of business mailing out last-date-of-service cancellations to stamp collectors across the nation.

A Tesnus signal maintainer had the responsibility of keeping his part of the Southern Pacific's tracks through the Big Bend in good order.

The post office ceased operation on June 15, 1954. The railroad razed all of the structures it had there, leaving only the siding. "Now," the former Tesnus resident said, "when someone asks where I am from, I normally tell them I am not from anywhere, because my hometown was torn down."

PROGRESS CITY

Progress City had a forward-sounding name for a new railroad town, but the only progress it ever saw came in the form of the money it made for its unscrupulous promoters.

No one ever drove a single nail into a single board in Progress City, which, legend has it, had been surveyed on undevelopable land atop 6,524-foot Sanitago Peak in Brewster County. As research published in the *Journal of Big Bend Studies* by Sul Ross State University geography professor Dr. Paul Wright has shown, the actual location of Progress City lay two miles to the northeast of the peak, not on top of it.

Half of the townsite actually did lie flat enough for construction (assuming that anyone could get to it), but the other half included the flank of the Sanitago Mountains, reaching an elevation of 4,747 feet. Regardless of its true coordinates, Progress City existed only in the imagination of the trusting buyers, hundreds of folks who shelled out money for town lots on a tract of land its owner had no intention of really developing.

Though merely one of numerous "sucker cities" platted and pedaled over the years across the arid Trans-Pecos, owning property in Progress City seemed like a good deal at the time. When lots went on sale in the late summer of 1909, the Kansas City, Mexico and Orient Railroad (better known simply as the Orient)—a line that would eventually extend from Missouri to Presidio and ultimately to the Pacific—had been surveyed as far as Fort Stockton, only fifty-eight miles from Marathon. And from Marathon it was only twenty-four miles to the site of Progress City. But the developers already knew that the line would be going from Fort Stockton to Alpine to Marfa to Presidio, a route no closer than forty-five miles to the townsite.

Still, right at the intersection of Twenty-third Street and Mitchell in Progress City, the plat said "Depot." Other planned amenities in Progress City included churches, a college, a school and a four-block town square.

Developers filed the plat map for Progress City with the Brewster County clerk on January 3, 1910, but lot sales had started the previous August. The townsite included 438 square blocks with twenty-four lots per block. W.L. Jackson of Atlanta in Cass County had been the first owner of a lot. Many others soon ponied up money to get in on the ground floor with Jackson.

One would think that a company selling land in Brewster County would have an office in Brewster County. But the Progress City Townsite Company officed on Herring Avenue in Waco, which, depending on the route taken, was at least 435 miles to Marathon.

Lee R. Davis was listed as owner and secretary of the company, with John L. Mauk serving as president. Davis was one of eight children of Lee and Catherine Davis, a couple with deep Texas roots. His father had fought during the Texas Revolution; his mother was the daughter of Neil McLennan, namesake of McLennan County. The elder Lee had been dead since 1867, but Catherine lived until 1905. Nine years before her death, in 1894 she and son Lee purchased land in Brewster County that would one day include the Progress City townsite. Almost immediately after acquiring the property, Catherine deeded her share to her son.

Big Bend historian Dr. Clifford Casey devoted several paragraphs to Progress City in his 1972 book *Mirages, Mysteries and Reality: Brewster County Texas*. "So many lots were sold in the 'sky-high city,'" he wrote, "that the District and County Clerks of Brewster County had special deed forms printed to facilitate the filing for record…In time there were so many…that two entire volumes of the Brewster County Deed Records were taken up with these deeds, with a total of over two thousand having been recorded."

The deeds show most Progress City lots were 25 by 120 feet and cost $1.50. Unfortunately, one lot was too narrow to build a house on, so most people usually bought more than one lot. The price for two adjacent lots ran $11.50.

Eventually, the developers moved 2,766 lots and took in $5,963 in sales—even after expenses, a decent living in the first decade of the twentieth century. In analyzing the deeds, Wright found that multiple sales would be made in one county in one day. That led him to theorize that the developers had hawked their land from county to county. Indeed, a website with more than one hundred searchable digitalized Texas newspapers reveals no paid advertising for Progress City. If they did any advertising, Davis and Mauk only placed ads in community newspapers before their sales visits.

How quickly Progress City property owners learned that no progress had been made on the town—and that none would be—is open to conjecture, but Brewster County authorities caught on to the scam fairly quickly. Even though the county made money in filing fees and stood to glean some tax revenue from Progress City landowners, on February 8, 1910, a local grand jury issued a report calling Davis out for scamming good citizens in other parts of the state and doing "great harm to the reputation of the area when duped persons discover the fraud." Grand jurors asked in the document that a copy of their report be sent to the district courts in Waco and to the Post Office Department but admitted that nothing much could be done legally about the fraudulent sales scheme.

Davis and Mauk skated, but the grand jury report and subsequent newspaper publicity poisoned their golden goose. Sales withered faster than range conditions during a bad drought. Six years later, the Brewster County Commissioner's Court removed Progress City from the tax rolls and formally declared the town plat null and void, noting that "there are no citizens living in the so called Progress City, that it is situated on a high mountain [inaccessible] to any one going on same far from habitation, [and] that the nearest anyone lives to said site is four miles."

Despite his distinguished Texas pedigree, Davis does not seem to have left deep footprints. His name seldom, if ever, made the public prints. Whether he ever got convicted in some other scam is not known, but one piece of circumstantial evidence—his name listed as a reference in a large newspaper ad touting an oil company drilling near Commerce in northeast Texas in 1919—suggests that he kept at it, finding new suckers for new schemes during the Texas oil boom.

Landmarks

Ernst Tinaja

The campers moved carefully up the draw in the moonlight, their flashlight beams crisscrossing the white limestone base of the narrow wash as they checked for any rattlesnakes that might be out and about looking for something to eat.

While being bitten by a rattlesnake is a serious medical matter that sometimes proves fatal, something much deadlier lay ahead in the darkness. Finally, they stood looking down into a geologic feature in Big Bend National Park called Ernst Tinaja, a deep natural water hole dug out of the rock over the millennia by erosion—a place of beauty tainted by a history of death.

"Tinaja" is a Spanish word meaning big, earthen jar. "Ernst" honors one Max A. Ernst, a German who came to the United States in 1873 and in 1884 moved to Pecos County in West Texas. Six years later, he gained American citizenship. Settling in Alpine in 1890, he leased a section of land around the landmark tinaja in southeastern Brewster County in 1898.

On land overlooking one of Tornillo Creek's eastern branches, along the ore road from Boquillas to Marathon, Ernst opened a store to cater to the miners and prospectors in the area. He built a one-room school near his store, and in 1903 he succeeded in getting the post office moved to his store from Boquillas. By then the community he had founded was known as La Noria ("the well"). In addition to being postmaster, he served as justice of the peace, county commissioner, school board trustee and notary public. For all practical purposes, Ernst was a one-man local government.

Located roughly a mile and a half east of Rio Grande Village (formerly known as Boquillas), or some eighteen miles from the park headquarters at Panther Junction, Ernst Tinaja is a timeless deathtrap. When brim-full, it is easy enough for an animal to satisfy its thirst along its rim. But when the water level is low, any creature jumping into the cool water for a drink or a refreshing swim will likely never leave. That's because the smooth limestone offers no purchase, especially when it's wet. A frantic animal—or human—would not even be able to cling to the side, much less scale the tinaja's slippery wall. As soon as exhaustion sets in, the hapless prisoner of the tinaja sinks and drowns.

Over the years, soldiers, ranchers, naturalists and, later, recreational hikers have occasionally found the carcass of a javelina, coyote or some other animal putrefying in the water, having floated to the surface as the decomposition process progresses. Roland Wauer, who spent years as the park's chief naturalist, once found a dead mountain lion in the tinaja. The tinaja is known to have killed at least one man and perhaps others in the time before recorded history.

For a time during the Mexican Revolution, the U.S. Army stationed a detachment of cavalry at La Noria. On August 19, 1913, Private Morton L. Diedel, a trooper in Company A of the Fourteenth Cavalry, asked a fellow soldier to join him in taking a bath at the tinaja. The soldier declined, but Diedel talked his friend Creed H. Mars into joining him. On their way there from camp, Diedel told Mars that he could not swim, and Mars admitted that he wasn't a very good swimmer himself. They took a dip in one of the smaller, shallower tinajas along the draw, got dressed and were headed back to their camp when Diedel slipped and fell into the big tinaja. Diedel said something that Mars couldn't hear but quickly disappeared under the water. Realizing that he'd probably get in trouble if he jumped in, too, Mars ran back to the camp for help. At first, the soldiers tried to bale out the tank, but finally someone who could swim jumped in and retrieved the body. Acting as coroner, the local justice of the peace conducted an inquest. After talking with several other soldiers, the JP concluded that Mars was telling the truth and had no complicity in the death, which he ruled an accidental drowning.

The tinaja also seemed to attract violent death. On September 27, 1908, Justice of the Peace Ernst, on his way back to his place at La Noria from Boquillas, stopped to open a wire fence gate on the road leading from the

Ernst Tinaja in Big Bend National Park. *Photo by Mike Cox.*

river to Marathon. A .44-caliber bullet slammed into his back and blew out below his stomach. Despite his wound, Ernst managed to get back on his horse and ride about two miles before his intestines began protruding from the exit wound. He dismounted and staggered over to a Spanish dagger plant, sitting down in its shade and hoping that someone would soon come by. Knowing that he was probably going to die, Ernst scribbled seventeen words on the back of an envelope: "Am shot, I expect by one of the Solis at gate. First shot hit two more missed."

A neighbor found the wounded judge and took him to his house, where he died the next day. In going through his pockets, Rosa Ernst found the written declaration made by her husband. That document, along with the well-known fact that Martin Solis's store at Boquillas had been adversely affected by the success of Ernst's store at La Noria, focused suspicion on Solis and his family. The following month, a Brewster County grand jury heard evidence in the case but did not hand down any indictments in connection with the murder. The investigation went on for three years, but no one ever faced trial in the matter.

Twenty-six-year-old Juan de Leon may have been on his way to or from the big tinaja when someone shot and killed him along the trail leading up to the water hole on July 19, 1932. Not found until several days later, he was buried where he died, his murder also unsolved. A concrete cross marks his rock-covered grave. The simple monument bears an equally simple epitaph: "E.P.D." (*En Paz Descanse*, "Rest in Peace.")

SAN ESTEBAN SPRINGS

As the twentieth century began its second decade, Americans thought that they could do anything, even transform part of the Chihuahuan Desert into a lush agricultural region. After all, engineers had raised the grade level of the entire city of Galveston and built a massive concrete and granite seawall to protect it from hurricanes. And in Panama, work proceeded apace on a canal that would connect the Atlantic with the Pacific.

Compared with those two public projects, building a dam across a wide draw eleven miles south of Marfa in Presidio County looked entirely doable. Rancher W.W. Bogel and other investors organized the Saint Stephen Land and Irrigation Company, and in 1910 construction began.

By July 15, 1911, workers had completed a reinforced concrete dam that stood nearly seven stories high and extended 669 feet across Alamita

Marfa, Texas

PRESIDIO COUNTY

Great Dam to Irrigate Rich Soil of San Esteban Valley

SANFORD J. TRUMAN, General Sales Manager
St. Stephen Land and Irrigation Co.
MARFA, TEXAS

Promoters of the new dam placed this large ad in the *San Antonio Express*.

San Esteban Springs. *Photo by Mike Cox.*

Creek and Antelope draws. The structure would corral the floodwater of a drainage area covering 450 square miles, creating a 3,100-acre lake with an average depth of 35 feet. In a land that only sees an average of nine inches of rain a year, the irrigation company may as well have created an ocean.

In addition to the dam, the company hired miners from the silver mine at Shafter to build an irrigation canal downhill from the dam to an expansive flat of dark volcanic soil that the developers envisioned as a veritable Garden of Eden. Depending on the terrain, water from the lake coursed through a mine-like tunnel, a rock-walled canal and, at one point, via a long galvanized flume.

A half-page ad in the *San Antonio Express* soon touted the "Great Dam" and the agricultural bounty it would bring. The Orient Railroad then under construction would pass through the property on its way to Presidio, creating a fast, inexpensive means of getting produce to market. Two new towns were planned to accommodate the influx of farmers who could buy irrigated land for eighty dollars per acre, one thousand acres minimum. "The man with the hoe will soon take a great deal of land which was formerly used for grazing purposes only," the newspaper ad declared.

While the San Esteban Valley fell somewhat short of becoming another San Joaquin Valley, the lake filled. People bought lots around its edge and built cabins and boat docks. Before long, bream, bass and catfish swam below as sailboats and motorized craft plied the water above.

Below the dam that made all of that possible trickled a series of five seeps collectively known as San Esteban Springs. As evidenced by prehistoric pictographs found nearby, the rock-wrapped water hole has been drawing human and animal visitors for millennia. Spanish explorers stopped there, as did Indians, soldiers, freighters traveling the Chihuahua Trail and others. For a time there was even a small community nearby variously known as Plata (Spanish for "silver") or San Esteban. The first rancher to own the springs and the land around it was Jim Ellison. Bogel, who acquired land along Alamita Creek in 1884 to raise sheep on, bought the San Esteban property in 1901 after switching to cattle raising.

When the Saint Stephen Land and Irrigation Company gave up on the project, the lake and an easement to it was conveyed to a Marfa-based organization called the San Esteban Lake Club. Access was for members only, though church and civic groups were welcome for free. In 1935, the club staged a regatta at the lake. Events included motorboat races, a sailboat race, a rowboat race and various swimming competitions. The annual event continued until World War II.

In a long-forgotten tragedy, three teenagers drowned in the lake on February 3, 1936, after their sailboat capsized. It took hundreds of searchers nearly a week to find their bodies. The incident gave rise to a legend that the owner of the property encompassing the lake dynamited the dam so that no one else would ever again die in its waters, but that was only a story, no matter how poignant sounding.

The dam withstood several floods, but its engineers apparently had not considered the problem of siltation. As the years went by, the lake held less and less water as its bottom became covered with mud. And in dry years, it held no water at all.

In 1944, with the lake empty, the club sold the property to C.A. Duncan of San Angelo with a provision that no water could be let out of the lake for irrigation purposes for twenty years. Duncan also agreed to lease the lake back to a reorganized club for the same period of time. With money raised by membership sales, the club hoped to mitigate the siltation problem by altering drainage patterns so that water would only flow into the impoundment from grassland. But since grassland depends on rain, wet and dry cycles continued to play havoc with the lake.

The infamous 1950s Texas drought dried it up again, but by the early 1960s the lake had refilled. On June 15, 1961, the *Alpine Avalanche* published a photograph of three men and a boy with nearly two hundred pounds of channel catfish caught in the lake. But with the development of larger, more stable lakes elsewhere in the state, interest in the off-again, on-again impoundment began to wane.

The lake is now owned by Betty Macguire, whose late husband acquired the ranch surrounding it in 1992. David Williams has been manager of the ranch since then.

Except for the dam, and the concrete foundations where waterfront cabins used to stand, it's hard to imagine that there ever was a lake. "This place hasn't had a big rain since 1996," Williams said. And that's the last time he's seen it with any water in it.

In the draw below the dam are several shallow caves in the rock bluffs, with piled rocks partially blocking their entrances. "We believe these shelters have multiple cultural layers," said Roger Boren, an archaeologist with the Center for Big Bend Studies at Sul Ross State University in Alpine. "Paleo people, Indians, the laborers who worked on the dam and irrigation system and track layers from when the Orient Railroad came through in 1920 all probably used them."

Williams has allowed Boren and other archeologists access to the ranch, which despite scientific examination still has its secrets. One of those mysteries is the origin of two dry-stacked stone buildings adjacent to the road leading to the springs.

"Take your pick as to who built them," Williams said. "They could be part of the old town of San Esteban, or they could have been a stage station along the Chihuahua Trail or built later." About a mile below the dam stands an L-shaped adobe ranch house that Bogel had built in the 1890s. Originally three bedrooms with a kitchen-dining room, over the years it has been expanded and the porch walled in. On the mantel over the fireplace is a reminder of better days: a blowup of a vintage black-and-white photo showing someone fishing from the top of the dam and a lady posing on one of the big rocks below.

Alpine's Holland Hotel

On June 19, 1941, a cross-country traveler who had spent the night at Alpine's Holland Hotel picked up a black-and-white postcard in the drugstore adjacent to the lobby and mailed it to a relative. While the sender's scribbled message amounted to nothing out of the ordinary, a promotional blurb printed on the card did a good job of summing up the venerable Big Bend hostelry in a catchy way:

The Largest Hotel
In the Largest City
In the Largest County
In the Largest State
In the Largest Group of States
In the World

While all of that could not be disputed, the Holland had only seventy rooms—certainly no giant. But beyond being a comfortable overnight stop for motorists passing through on U.S. Highway 90, a major east–west route, the hotel stood as the social center of the Big Bend. Cattlemen drank coffee and made deals there, Alpine's civic clubs gathered there each week and the hotel's ballroom accommodated chamber of commerce dinners, dances, wedding receptions and other events.

Brewster County rancher John Holland built the hotel in 1912 at the corner of Sixth Street and the broad thoroughfare that bears his name, just across from the town's railroad depot. Though Alpine had neither dikes nor tulips, in pondering what to name his new inn, Holland

Alpine's Holland Hotel during its heyday.

thought that Holland Hotel seemed imminently suitable. Holland's son, Clay, took over management of the hotel when the elder Holland died and had it renovated in 1923, adding a third story and bathrooms in each room.

"[The Holland] is so thoroughly equipped that it will do credit to cities many times the size of Alpine, and the traveling public are invariably surprised as the advantage enjoyed at this modern hostelry," bragged the *Marfa New Era* in its March 1924 Big Bend edition. "No one enterprise in this part of Texas has given to this city, and to this part of the Southwest, more favorable publicity nationally than has the Holland Hotel. No trip through this section is complete without a stay at the Holland, and without question one of the pleasantest memories of the journey is the time spent at this hotel."

Three years later, Holland thoroughly transformed the hotel, adding a three-story addition. Designed in the Spanish Colonial style by noted El Paso architect Henry C. Trost (his credits also include Marfa's Hotel Paisano and Van Horn's El Capitan Hotel), the new building cost $250,000. According to a special edition of the *Alpine Avalanche* published to celebrate the hotel's March 16, 1928 reopening, the Holland had "common battery telephone service, and many other modern conveniences."

The newspaper praised Clay Holland for "his progressive move in building a hotel which should be the pride of the whole community." For his part, Holland believed that he had made a sound investment. "Few people realize just how good a town we have here and what the future has in store for it," he said.

By the end of World War II, American travel tastes had begun to change. Railroads saw fewer and fewer passengers as automobiles became the nation's primary mode of transportation. Tourists liked the convenience of motels, where they could park right in front of their room, unload their bags and then head for the motel swimming pool. With business declining, Clay Holland sold the hotel in 1946.

A year later, the hotel's new owner got the kind of publicity that no innkeeper wants. On March 20, 1947, a married woman armed with a handgun confronted the hotel's assistant manager in the lobby of the Holland and shot him five times. The woman left the man bleeding on the floor and went to her residence, where Brewster County sheriff Clarence Hord arrested her about an hour later and charged her with assault with intent to murder. The hotel employee survived, but whatever its nature, his relationship with the woman did not.

A few years later, Holland figured in a more upbeat news story. In June 1950, rancher Gene Cartledge presented hotel manager Frank Hofues with what he represented as an eaglet. The bird turned out to be a common blackbird, not the majestic and threatened American bald eagle, but Hofues made a pet out of it anyway. Named Blackie, the bird became one of the hotel's permanent guests. But during the day, he made his rounds around town, begging for food outside the Williams and Vogt grocery store and sipping suds at a nearby bar. The bird took particular pleasure in soaring toward some unsuspecting victim from behind, landing parrot-like on his or her shoulder. In April 1951, Blackie disappeared. Folks figured that he had gone off to answer the call of the wild, but in October he came back to the Holland. Hofues knew that it was Blackie because he still had the dab of white paint slapped on his tail by a maintenance worker he had annoyed. How long Blackie hung around the Holland after that went unreported.

Meanwhile, the hotel continued through a succession of owners until 1969. That year, the latest owner opted to shut down the hotel, selling off all of the furniture and equipment.

Gene Hendryx, local radio station owner and a member of the Texas House of Representatives, bought the shuttered hotel in 1972 and restored it for use as a combination hotel and office building. The Hendryx estate sold the building in 1985, and it again went through several owners. Jennifer and John Jones of Sonora bought the Holland in 2009 and did some substantial remodeling. "We want to share the architecture of a great hotel and become a cornerstone of this community," Jones told the *Avalanche*.

Michael Bazaar, who took over management of the hotel in the spring of 2011, said that the Joneses only own the 1928 section of the hotel. "We have twenty-four keys," he said. The original building across the patio to the east, fronting on Sixth Street, is owned by Cameron rancher Walter Pyle, who lives there and is converting it to apartments. Bazaar lives in San Antonio and commutes to the Holland via Amtrak. He also manages Alpine's Maverick Inn.

The Holland is no longer the largest hotel in Alpine, and Texas is no longer the largest state in the country, but it's still popular with visitors. The management even provides earplugs for guests who don't find the rumble and clatter of passing trains sleep inducing.

Rancho Valle de la Cienga

Part of L.A. Wilke's job as city editor of the scrappy *Fort Worth Press* was staying ahead of the competition, including the rival *Fort Worth Star-Telegram* and the dailies in Dallas, including the *Morning News*.

Perusing the *News* one morning in the spring of 1927 to see if any of his reporters had gotten scooped, Wilke read a short item reporting that silent film star Noah Berry, his wife and his son would be spending some time that summer at a new resort south of Alpine in Brewster County called Rancho Valle de la Cienga. Former Texas Ranger Pete Crawford, a well-known Big Bend area lawman, would be managing the dude ranch.

The resort would be opening that July, the article continued, "and a number of prominent people and celebrities have already made reservations at this popular resort, but have requested that no publicity be given as they desire to enjoy a vacation out of the lime light if possible."

While Wilke could understand that the stars might want a little peace and quiet, he knew that the owners of the ranch would probably be interesting in getting the word out about their property. Calling his friend, Ranger captain Tom Hickman, who commanded Fort Worth–based Company B, Wilke got Crawford's address and typed out a letter offering to write a feature story that would help publicize the place in exchange for a week's stay for his family. Crawford replied by telegraph that such a trade would be fine.

Old postcard view of Cathedral Mountain from Rancho Valle de la Cienga.

Founded in 1881 by Lawrence Haley, the forty-thousand-acre ranch lay about fifteen miles south of Alpine at the base of 5,100-foot Cathedral Mountain. When Haley died in 1917, his foreman, George Brown, inherited the property. A large adobe ranch house built around a quadrangle stood as the ranch's architectural centerpiece. A spring on the side of the mountain, where cottonwoods grew in the rich soil, provided water. The twenty-eight-by eighty-foot main hall had been used for mohair storage in the 1890s as the ranch weathered a national economic slump and corresponding drop in wool prices during Grover Cleveland's presidency. Oil from the wool had soaked into the wooden floor, giving it a unique finish. It had been cleaned and polished and, with the opening of the guest operation, used for a dance floor.

That summer of 1927, taking a couple weeks off for a working vacation, Wilke drove his family from Fort Worth to Corpus Christi and then on west to Alpine. Through a contest, he had won twenty four- by five-inch film packs from the Agfa Company, then just starting to do business in America. He took that film along to the Big Bend and shot numerous pictures.

In talking with Crawford and Brown, Wilke learned that the former ranger had suggested starting a dude ranch there several years before. But Brown had demurred, arguing that his ranch and its thousands of white-faced Herefords and sheep already made him a good enough living. The deadlock broke when Crawford promised to allow only guests "with a certain native understanding of how to comingle agreeably with their fellow men."

Beyond the striking mountain scenery, the ranch offered good grub, including chuck wagon cookouts, and twice-daily horseback rides. In between meals, guests could use the main room to play bridge or wile away their time sitting on the porch soaking in the view.

In addition to the newspaper piece that he would write on the guest ranch, Wilke pursued another story on a newly open wooden toll bridge between Presidio and Ojinaga. The old bridge between the two cities had burned, and a man from Brownwood had built the replacement. Always looking for a money-saving angle, Wilke worked a publicity deal with the contractor by which he would write a story on the new bridge for all of the major state papers in exchange for $100.

Crawford agreed to drive Wilke to Presidio. A cowboy Wilke remembered only as "Slick" joined them on the trip. They drove across ranches, with Crawford taking time out to shoot a coyote.

Former Texas Ranger Pete Crawford, *left*, and an unidentified rider take in the scenery at Rancho Valle de la Cienga.

While photographing the new bridge, they ran across the Mexican army general in charge in Ojinaga. Rather than a uniform, the officer wore trousers and a loud pink silk shirt, open at the collar. More than happy to pose for photographs, after the picture-taking, the general invited the Texans to cross over for a bit of hospitality. Wilke was a teetotaler, but the proposition suited Crawford and his cowboy pal just fine.

The general graciously bought the drinks. After the third or fourth round, the spirit of generosity seized "Slick," who insisted on picking up a round. He slapped his money down on the bar, but the pink-shirted general shoved it back, explaining that American money might as well be counterfeit in Mexico. The drunken Texan took that as an insult, and an international incident nearly developed. Before things got out of hand, Wilke and the ex-ranger finally got the cowboy calmed down, apologized to the general and drove back across the bridge to Presidio and from there returned to the guest ranch.

Wilke followed through on his promise to publicize both the new dude ranch and the bridge. He also told his friends what a fine time he and his family had at the ranch. One of those friends was Carl Mosig, a reporter for the *Dallas Morning News*.

"A newspaper man in Fort Worth who had discovered...Rancho Valle [de] la Cienga had urged me to visit Pete [Crawford] during my vacation.

He had rather raved about the place, about its beauty, its hospitality and especially about Pete. I now rave with him," Mosig wrote.

Mosig visited the ranch in the later summer of 1928. As soon as he could, he got Crawford off to the side for an interview. Sitting under a giant live oak tree on the working part of the ranch, the reporter and Crawford smoked cigarettes and talked. "I've wandered the West over from Canada to Mexico, from Kansas to California," Crawford said, "but partner, this stretch of country around Alpine is not only the best cattle country but the best looking lay-out in the lot."

The conversation soon took on a philosophical bent. "You city folks have a lot of things I don't have—street cars, tall buildings, paved streets," Crawford said after the reporter told him how much he admired the ranch. "But you also have a lot of worry, racket and a general spirit of unrest. It's a continual stampede with you."

The dude ranch was in business to make money, but Crawford said that "money-making" wasn't the most important thing in life, at least not to him. "I may be old-fashioned but this present-day fight for money that is the underlying spirit of all big cities would spoil my aim," he said. "It does something crippling to your insides if you keep it up too long."

After a trip to the city, Crawford continued, he always wanted to get back to Big Bend. As soon as he could, he said, he'd "saddle a horse and take myself a ride up the country to get back the feeling that life is pretty sweet after all."

Crawford's comments about the preoccupation with money proved prophetic. After Rancho Valle de la Cienga enjoyed one more robust tourist season in the summer of 1929, the stock market crashed in the fall. As the nation sank into a financial depression, Brown gave up on the resort and concentrated on keeping his ranch in business.

Big Bend Promoters

Touring a Future Park with a One-Armed Ranger

With one-armed Texas Ranger Arch Miller riding along as escort, the brand new Ford Model A bounced along the rough road leading into the old mining town Boquillas. D.E. Colp, chairman of the State Parks Board, sat behind the wheel.

An executive with the Uvalde Rock Asphalt Company, Colp had been Governor Pat Neff's initial appointee to the first State Parks Board. In fact, Colp *was* the board. This was his second visit to the Big Bend in a month.

Riding in the back seat were L.A. Wilke, city editor of the *Fort Worth Press*, and Harry Williams, a veteran writer for the *San Antonio Light*. Wilke had an assignment from the Cleveland-based Newspaper Enterprise Association, a syndicate operated by the Scripps-Howard newspaper chain, to write a feature story on the movement to develop a large state park in the Big Bend. Williams would be writing a story for his newspaper.

Wilke's wife, staying with her mother in San Angelo, was only a few weeks away from giving birth to their second child. That the Fort Worth newspaperman was about to become a father again may or may not have been a topic of conversation as the four men headed for the Rio Grande that early September day in 1928, but the topic of paternity did come up in another way. As they drove around Boquillas, Wilke noticed that all of the Mexican kids would gather by the roadside, stand briskly at attention and salute them as they drove by. "You'd better salute, you little bastards; I might be your daddy," the ranger chaperon would say.

Visiting the area in August, Colp had spoken to the Alpine Chamber of Commerce about the economic benefits that would come to the region with the development of better roadways. Colp said that a planned scenic highway through the Davis Mountains would be worth at least $1 million a year to the area. He said that the state also was working on establishing a state highway between Fort Stockton and Alpine. As for parks, he envisioned a series of small parks along the highway through the Davis Mountains.

The news hook for Colp's September Big Bend visit was the recent donation to the state of seven thousand acres by rancher John Humphries of Marfa. The Presidio County acreage was intended for development as a state park.

L.A. Wilke, city editor of the *Fort Worth Press*, about the time he toured the Big Bend to publicize the need for a park in the region.

Colp and Williams had driven from San Antonio to San Angelo, where Wilke joined them. It took them all morning to cover the 118 miles from San Angelo to the booming oil town of McCamey, where they stopped for lunch at a greasy spoon café full of roughnecks. After they ate, Williams asked for a glass of water to wash his false teeth. The request incensed the waitress. "A barrel of oil would be easier to get than water in this town," she told him. Williams cleaned his teeth with his handkerchief.

Wilke had gotten to know Colp in Fort Worth when he gave a talk there that Wilke covered for his newspaper. The park board chairman said that a good story could be done about the plans for a park in the Big Bend. Wilke queried the NEA about doing an illustrated story on the Big Bend and got a go-ahead. He would also write the story for his own newspaper.

From McCamey, the men preceded to Alpine, where they spent the night at the newly expanded Holland Hotel. The next morning, they drove south to the lower part of the Big Bend, where they followed the poor roads—more like trails—up the river to Boquillas. They spent the night at the ranger headquarters there, which is where they met Arch Miller.

They had lunch the next day at the trading post that Elmo Johnson had opened sixteen miles south of Castolon the year before. Wilke watched as a group of Mexicans came across the river with a string of burros loaded with candellia, a plant that could be reduced to wax. On his side of the river, Johnson grew corn and other truck.

From Johnson's ranch, they drove northwest to Marfa, where Wilke met store owner and Big Bend history buff Mrs. O.L. Shipman, daughter of former Texas Ranger captain Pat Dolan. She gave Wilke a copy of her new book, *Taming the Big Bend*. After leaving Marfa, the party headed to Presidio via the bustling silver mining town of Shafter. At Presidio, they met two U.S. Customs Service men, one named Orin Dow, the other a young man with an attractive wife who, Wilke later recalled, appeared to be "free with her favors." From Presidio, the customs agents escorted the party to a camp (a thatch-covered *jacal*) that they kept about forty miles from town. Dow later acquired a ranch in Mexico and became a successful cattleman and a respected citizen of El Paso.

The next day they were guests on L.C. Brite's ranch. Brite escorted them to one of the Big Bend's most beautiful and still least-seen features, the spring-fed Capote Falls, which drop 175 feet. They also met with Humphries at his ranch.

Later, in Santa Elena Canyon, they encountered four rough-and-tumble river fishermen. The men had planned to use chicken entrails to bait their trotlines, but they had either forgotten their bait or lost it. Happy to help some fellow anglers, Wilke used the .22 pistol he taken on the trip and went off and shot a couple of jackrabbits. He gave the rabbits to the fishermen, who gutted them and used their viscera to bait their trotlines. Wilke and Colp then hiked up the canyon for some distance. When they returned a couple of hours later, the trotline fishermen had a bunch of catfish on the line, thanks to the rabbit guts.

While following trails, they jumped a cougar in a salt cedar flat across the river. Wilke took several shots at it with a Marlin lever-action .22 rifle, believing that he may have hit it even though the cat paced a fair distance off and he had to shoot down hill. The cougar had come to the river for water.

When they got back to Alpine, the group broke up, and Wilke returned by train to San Angelo to pick up his wife and daughter. Back in Fort Worth, Wilke wrote his story on the Big Bend and was pleased to see that it appeared in other Scripps-Howard newspapers across the nation, another step in the movement to develop a national park in the region.

Jack Hoxie Saw Fort Davis as "Hollywood" East

Thirty-seven years after the army abandoned Fort Davis, a celluloid cowboy announced plans to convert the old cavalry post into a motion picture colony and resort. Unfortunately, he soon found out that timing is as important in real estate development as it is in lassoing a runaway steer.

Born in Indian Territory in 1885 well before Oklahoma statehood, John Hartford Hoxie started out as a cowboy, took up rodeoing and in 1913 landed a role in a silent western called *The Tragedy of Big Eagle Mine*. Soon billing himself as Jack Hoxie, throughout the rest of the decade and well into the 1920s the stocky, cleft-chinned cowboy starred in scores of flickering horse operas. His biggest hit came when he played Buffalo Bill in *The Last Frontier*, a pre-sound blockbuster released in 1926.

But as Hollywood moved on to "talkies," producers discovered that while Hoxie had a good voice, he couldn't remember his lines. Thus tarnished, his star status had begun to fade by 1929. That's the year he decided that the Big Bend country of Texas would make a good location for another shot at the big time.

In April 1929, Hoxie rented the property where old Fort Davis stood and announced plans to transform it into the Hoxie Stockade and Motion

Picture Studio. The officers' quarters would be restored to accommodate tourists coming to enjoy a large swimming pool, a polo field, a golf course, tennis courts, a dance pavilion, a rodeo arena and more. A month later, Hoxie hit Fort Davis and invited local folks to join him in the venture, signing up investors at $100 a share.

Though only two of the twelve officers' quarters had been renovated by the following spring, Hoxie did succeed in bringing 3,500 or so visitors to Fort Davis on March 23, 1930, for a rodeo touted as featuring six Hollywood "Cowboys and Cowgirls." While spectators got to see some trick riding and roping, a severe dust storm ended the show before it had hardly begun.

That proved to be only the beginning of a run of bad luck for Hoxie and his dream of making Fort Davis into Hollywood East. With the economy continuing to worsen following the October 1929 stock market crash,

Silent movie star Jack Hoxie envisioned a restored Fort Davis, but that didn't happen until the old post became a National Historic Site in the 1960s. *Photo by Mike Cox.*

Hoxie's financial backing dried up faster than a cow patty in July. Not long after the fizzled rodeo, Hoxie stored what tack and furnishings he had acquired, hired a caretaker for the fort and left town to perform with the 101 Wild West Show.

The year 1931 did not prove any better of a year for Hoxie. The actor's private Pullman car, owned by showman C.G. Dodson, caught on fire at the Missouri-Pacific rail yard in San Antonio in the early morning of January 2, 1931. No one had been in the car at the time, but the fire gutted the $20,000 Pullman.

Only three weeks later, three of Hoxie's associates in the Fort Davis venture generated some highly unfavorable publicity in Midland. On January 25, western actor and former Texas Ranger Buck Jones, movie producer Bert Bennet and Lee Cox, a former Sul Ross College student who had gone to work for Hoxie, enlivened a party thrown by oil field driller Oscar Yates and his wife in honor of her brother. As the party wound down, likely following the ingestion of much nonpetroleum lubrication on the part of Jones, the cowboy pulled a .38-caliber pistol. Yates told him to put it away, to which Jones replied, "I have had twenty-five years' experience with these things." And then the handgun discharged.

Weldon R. Russell, an Abilene real estate man, collapsed with a bullet in his intestines. At first, the partygoers thought that Jones had pulled a Hollywood stunt, but then someone opened Russell's coat and saw real blood. With the guests in "the wildest confusion," Jones and Cox left Yates's house and sped off in Jones's car. Arrested some hours later in Stanton, the two were returned to Midland, where Jones was charged with murder and Cox held as a material witness. Russell died in a Midland hospital the following afternoon.

The only favorable publicity Hoxie got that year came in February, when the *San Antonio Express* carried a story about a black bear named "Dynamite" that Hoxie kept at Fort Davis. When the year-old female awakened from her winter hibernation on February 22, 1931, Hoxie and animal trainer Bert DeMarc brought her a tub of water and a quart of cornmeal mixed with water. "She licked the platter clean, boxed it 40 feet aside with her paw, hopped upon the top of her den and gave herself a good scratching," the newspaper reported on what must have been a slow news day.

Not mentioned in the story was that while Hoxie's bear had ended her seasonal snooze, the film star's plans for a Big Bend resort continued in hibernation. With the Great Depression deepening, Hoxie soon rode out of town on the figurative horse he had come in on. In the fall of 1932, his wife, Dixie Starr, returned just long enough to take possession of all of the trunks of costumes and boxes of tack left behind and take them back to California. Left holding the proverbial bag, dozens of Jeff Davis County investors never got their money back.

Hoxie continued to perform in rodeos for another twenty years, but his career had peaked decades before. The old actor did a slow ride toward the sunset, dying of leukemia at eighty on March 28, 1965, in Elkhart, Kansas.

Unlike his sure-shooting movie persona, over the course of his long life Hoxie missed many of the real-life targets he had taken a shot at. But when it came to recognizing a good movie location, he had hit the bull's eye with Fort Davis, even if he never knew it. Long after Hoxie's Stockade and Motion Picture Studio had been forgotten, Hollywood did come to Fort Davis in the 1990s, using the old fort and the area landscape as the scenic backdrop for two moderately successful films, *The Good Old Boys* and *Dancer, Texas.*

Getting There and Back

"The Sun Has Riz, the Sun Has Set"

Texas and the rest of the nation struggled in the economic chaos of the Great Depression that July 1931 when the Southern Pacific Lines printed its latest timetables for Texas and Louisiana. In parentheses below the date were the words "Destroy Previous Issues." Fortunately, whoever once owned the copy found more than six decades later for sale in an antique store didn't comply with the railroad's directive. Sure, the times listed in the thirty-two-page, coat pocket–sized brochure may have been "Subject to Change Without Notice," but they make for interesting reading today.

When the SP distributed its latest timetable that long-ago spring, four passenger trains a day passed through the upper Big Bend on their way back and forth between the two coasts. Trains 103 and 101 of the Sunset Limited headed west each day, while Trains 102 and 104 raced through on their way east.

Except for Sanderson, Marathon, Alpine, Marfa and Valentine, the trains passed through places that even then were mostly just names on a map. From Sanderson heading west, this was the itinerary: Gavilan, Emerson, Longfellow, Rosenfeld, Maxon, Tesnus, Haymond, Warwick, Marathon, Lenox, Altuda, Strobel, Alpine, Toronto, Paisano, Nopal, Marfa, Galgo, Aragon, Conejo, Ryan, Quebec and Valentine. Of those places, Longfellow, Rosenfeld, Tesnus, Haymond and Paisano were flag stops. Sanderson, Longfellow, Tesnus, Marathon, Alpine and Marfa had telegraph service.

When the railroad first traversed the Big Bend in the early 1880s, only Haymond, Marathon, Alpine and Marfa (in east–west order) had passenger and freight depots. The stations in each town all looked alike—two-story structures built of redwood to standard company specifications. Of those, the stations at Marfa and Alpine saw the most traffic.

A Southern Pacific timetable issued in 1932 that lists passenger trains crossing the Big Bend.

Alpine's original depot lasted until December 15, 1901, when a fire destroyed it. The SP rebuilt on the same site but this time used a different cookie-cutter plan to put up only a one-story depot. That was the building still in use when the railroad published its spring 1931 schedule.

According to that schedule, Sunset Limited Train Number 101, westbound, hit the Texas state line at the Sabine River about 5:20 a.m., arriving in Houston three hours later. After only ten minutes to unload and load passengers and mail, the train continued its journey westward. Continuing on through San Antonio, the train finally pulled into Alpine at 1:25 p.m. the following day. By 6:30 p.m., more than twenty-five hours after crossing Texas's eastern boundary, the train slowed to a stop at El Paso's Union Station. That it took more than a day for a fast passenger train to make it through the Lone Star state gave rise to a popular postcard rhyme:

The sun has riz
The sun has set
Here we is
In Texas yet

The Sunset Limited still carries passengers to and from the Big Bend, although much has changed since 1931. The biggest change is that SP has been out of business for decades; it and other passenger providers were replaced by Amtrak, which began operations on May 1, 1971. The second biggest change is that it costs a lot more to take the train than it used to. And finally, now only one train a day slides into the depot at Alpine (its only Big Bend stop), and that's only three times a week each way.

The depot the SP built in Alpine in 1902 made it until a snowy January night in 1946 when, once again, fire necessitated a new station. This time, the railroad built a station of concrete blocks covered with stucco in the Mission Southwest style. That depot is still in use. Of nineteen Amtrak stations in Texas, only four are less busy than Alpine, where the average number of daily passengers is eleven.

One thing that's as timely today as it was in 1931 is the slogan that appeared on the bottom of each page of the timetable: "Go By Train—Save Time-Money-Energy." Of course, it's debatable whether whoever crafted that slogan saw "energy" as meaning what it does in the twenty-first century.

McDonald Observatory VIPs Trapped in Orbit

For hundreds of years, man has depended on the regularity of the earth's rotation, the moon's cycles and the movement of the stars and planets as the basis for our calculation of time and the structure of our calendar. Still, scientists understand that the universe can be as chaotic as it is predictable.

On November 26, 1968, astronomers from around the world, University of Texas faculty and high-ranking staff, state and federal elected officials, National Aeronautics and Space Administration representatives and assorted other invitees flew to Marfa and then traveled by chartered bus to McDonald Observatory near Fort Davis for the dedication of a new 107-inch telescope.

For at least one of the visitors, the trip to the observatory atop the sugarloaf-shaped Mount Locke amounted to history repeating itself. In 1939, as executive secretary of the El Paso County Board of Development,

The McDonald Observatory shortly after it opened in 1939.

L.A. Wilke had traveled from El Paso to attend the dedication of the first McDonald telescope. Now, nearly three decades later, he was on hand for the 1968 event.

Wilke well-remembered the first dedication. The Southern Pacific Railroad, which cut through the upper Big Bend via Marathon, Alpine and Marfa, ran numerous "Dedication Special" trains to Marfa, the nearest station to Fort Davis and the then new observatory.

Scientists from all over the world packed the sixty-foot-diameter dome to listen to various presentations by their learned colleagues. After a morning of ceremony and talk, the visitors enjoyed a chuck wagon–style barbecue lunch, followed by a series of rodeo performances put together by the nearby Prude Ranch. More speechifying followed.

The 1939 dedication received national and international media attention for several reasons. For one, the new observatory had a catchy backstory. A bachelor banker from Paris, Texas, who knew a lot about money but little of astronomy believed that the study of heavenly bodies would lead to improved meteorological forecasting for farmers. Accordingly, in his will W.J. McDonald bequeathed $850,000 to the University of Texas to fund an observatory. Once a legal challenge to the will had been overcome, since UT had no astronomy faculty, it entered into an agreement with the University of Chicago to operate the planned new observatory for thirty years.

A close-up of McDonald Observatory in 1955. *Photo by L.A. Wilke.*

The second thing that made the 1939 dedication important was the size of McDonald's telescope. It would be eighty-two inches, the second largest in the world at the time. By the mid-1960s, UT had a well-established astronomy program and took over operation of the observatory it had always owned.

Planning for a larger telescope began in 1964, and by early 1965 the necessary mirror blanks had been ordered. A year later, work began on assembling the telescope, and building a second mountain top dome was well underway by 1967. When completed, the new Harlan J. Smith Telescope ranked as the third largest in the world.

For the 1968 dedication, UT chartered a Braniff International airliner to fly all of the VIPs to Marfa, which had a still usable World War II–era runway sufficient for an Electra four-engine propjet. That worked fine in getting to Marfa, but following the morning's ceremonies, the universe's less predictable side took over.

First it started raining, which is unusual enough meteorological behavior for the Chihuahuan Desert in winter. Then, as a particularly strong cold front overrode an unusual amount of moisture, it started sleeting, followed by snow.

Still, the Braniff pilot thought that he could make it out of Marfa on schedule at 2:15 p.m. But as he taxied down the runaway, the plane plowed up a spray of snow, its left wheel soon sinking into a slushy pothole. No one had been hurt, but the plane clearly wasn't going to get off the ground that afternoon. "They took us off the plane, said they were sorry and brought us back to the hotel," Wilke recalled.

A quickly developed Plan B involved busing the VIPs to Midland's airport for another Braniff flight, but the state highway patrol had shut down the snow-covered roads. Plan C was to bus everyone back to Austin, but again the roads were too bad, even though one bus with students and some faculty members did make it out at about 5:30 p.m. "The old folks decided not to try to get on that one," Wilke said.

With just about every UT official except Chancellor Harry Ransom stuck in tiny Marfa, some wag in the group suggested that the town be renamed the "University of Texas at Marfa."

Finally, Plan D: UT would buy everyone a train ticket to San Antonio. So, at 9:50 p.m., the daily eastbound Sunset Limited pulled out of the Marfa station with some sixty tired VIPs facing an all-night train ride before reaching the Alamo City at 10:15 a.m.

Despite the inconvenience, the group had not been undone by the surprise snowstorm, which dropped half a foot of snow on Marfa and ended up covering most of west Texas under a near-record (for fall) blanket of white.

One of the VIPs stranded by the surprise snowstorm was L.A. Wilke, who nearly thirty years earlier had attended the first McDonald Observatory dedication.

The mostly forgotten incident proved to be the last hurrah for the venerable Sunset Limited, at least as a privately operated passenger train. Only six months earlier, having lost nearly $1 million on the route in 1968, the Southern Pacific Railroad had filed notice with the Interstate Commerce Commission that it planned to discontinue passenger service.

"I remember when there used to be signs along the highway that said 'Next Time Take a Train,'" Wilke said. "The signs are gone, and the trains nearly are…but I can see the point."

Johnny Newell's Road Logs

Long before the Internet, long before "Google" became a verb and long before the marriage of the words "search" and "engine," anyone planning on visiting the Big Bend had to invest some effort to acquire travel information—especially if they wanted to know anything about all the vast landscape between point A and B, as in Alpine and Big Bend National Park. Either that or pick up a free copy of Johnny Newell's "Newell–Gulf Road Log."

Starting in 1965 and continuing into the 1980s, Newell bankrolled, researched, wrote, produced, distributed and promoted a set of twenty-two single sheet road logs available to anyone traveling in Texas west of the Pecos. He even took in a little territory east of the Pecos.

Born in Carthage, Missouri, in 1907 to wandering parents, Newell lived in fifteen states before enrolling in Princeton University. Graduating magna cum laude and as a member of Phi Beta Kappa with a geology degree in 1929, Newell went to Europe for a while to practice his new profession. Back in the States, he married Bonnie Boone in 1930, and the couple moved to Texas, where he worked as a geologist in the oil fields. But by then the nation had drifted into the worst economic depression in its history, forcing Newell to become possibly the best educated gas jockey in the Lone Star state. Pumping gas at a Houston service station, he worked ten-hour days with no days off for seventy-two dollars a month.

Permanently abandoning the exploration side of the oil industry for the distribution end of the business, Newell took over the Trans-Pecos sales territory as a jobber for Gulf Oil. Arriving in Alpine in 1939 with R.F. Schermerhorn, he started the Newell Oil Company.

In addition to making a good living, Newell got to see firsthand the development of Big Bend National Park. Realizing that tourism both sold more gasoline for Gulf and benefited the local economy, he spent most of the rest of his life promoting the region as a travel destination and through various civic endeavors, trying to make it a better place for those who already lived there.

Newell's unique series of road logs trace to a summer evening in 1965. Standing in the lobby of a motel in Del Rio, the affable Newell struck up a conversation with an Indiana tourist who had spent most of the day driving the 425 miles from El Paso. Most boring drive he'd ever made, the Hoosier motorist complained to Newell.

While no one could argue that the man had not driven a long way, Newell couldn't understand how the visitor could have found his trip uninteresting. After all…and then, in his mind, he started ticking off all of the points of interest he knew about along that route: old cavalry forts, abandoned mines, ghost towns, mile-high mountains, an old railroad bridge about to be drowned by a new dam and so on. None of those things seemed boring to Newell, and he believed that most other people would see it the same way. Of course, they had to know what they were driving by.

Johnny Newell presents a Big Bend visitor with a copy of one of his road logs.

A few days after his encounter with the tourist, Newell recruited a friend to ride shotgun and take notes, set the trip meter of his car to 0 at Del Rio's Civic Center and headed toward his home in Alpine. En route he dictated notes regarding interesting features and stories along the way, calling out the mileage of each point. Maybe it was Newell's background as an oil field geologist that made him think of "road log" as opposed to "road guide," but that's how he got started in the tourist information field.

Newell paid for the printing out of his own pocket and gave the logs away, stocking them in every Gulf station in west Texas, at more than 150 motels and at the visitor centers operated by the state Highway Department. Possibly to guard against someone trying to sell the logs—or perhaps just to underscore the point—each sheet had the word "Free" on it six times.

"This type of road load is a new idea," he wrote on his logs in 1967, "and we'd sort of like to know what you think of it." Newell invited mail, and as his logs became better known and saw more and more use by travelers, he got plenty of positive feedback.

Within a few years, Newell had produced a set of twenty-two different logs, a "heading to" or "leaving from" log for each of various routes across the Trans-Pecos, including the El Paso to Del Rio drive that got the whole thing started. Other routes described the long stretch from Sonora to El Paso, Midland-Odessa to El Paso and the two main routes into Big Bend National Park. Initially, Newell had the logs mimeographed (the stencil-and-ink forerunner of photocopying) but later got them printed on legal-sized paper. Each log bore a number followed by either "E" or "W" for east and west or "N" or "S" for the other two cardinal directions.

It's clear to anyone reading his logs that Newell was passionate about the "W" side of the state. At the end of his eastbound Fort Stockton–Sonora log, he wrote: "Sorry, but this is the end of the Newell–Gulf Road log route. When you come back west, stop at any Gulf Station in Sonora, Ozona, Midland, Odessa, or Del Rio to start your…trip across the Trans-Pecos."

For someone who had such a profound impact on Big Bend tourism, Newell and his innovative road logs got surprisingly little attention in the news media over the years. The *Alpine Avalanche* put his name in the paper a lot, but that was because he had served as president of the chamber of commerce and on the Texas Good Neighbor Commission, as well as was active in the Rotary Club and numerous other civic endeavors.

But humorist H. Allen Smith, a prolific professional writer who came to Alpine from New York late in his life, knew a good story when he saw one

Navigating the Big Bend hasn't always been easy. Obviously with plenty of time on his hands, someone took this photograph between Alpine and Fort Davis in 1922.

and interviewed Newell for a piece in *Texas Parade*, a magazine that went out of business not long after *Texas Monthly* first hit the newsstands in 1975.

Newell continued to update his logs throughout most of the 1970s. He died on November 27, 1980, and is buried in Alpine's Elm Grove Cemetery. One thing Newell never did was consolidate all of his logs into book form, a publication that would have done well. Today, surviving copies of the logs are rarer than full-service gas stations and are nowhere to be found online.

Though a lot of work went into keeping the logs up to date, it's evident in reading them that Nevell had fun doing them. "You'll enjoy your trip more when you know what you're seeing," he liked to say, a line he reduced to a standard subhead on each sheet. But at the end of the last eastbound log, he confessed: "It's been quite a job climbing all those mountains to measure the elevation and counting all the people in those towns, but we've enjoyed it and we hope you have, too."

Laughing Matters

Just a "Little Side Show"

Old-time Texans enjoyed practical jokes more than their descendants, it seems. Maybe it's fear of litigation, but these days good-natured tricks are about as scarce as jobs or easy credit.

One frigid day in 1889, a gang of hoboes descended on barely five-year-old Alpine. In the words of iconoclastic newspaper writer-publisher John S. "K. Lamity" Bonner, who heard the tale from a witness and retold it years later in his monthly *K. Lamity's Harpoon*, the bums arrived in Brewster County's principal town "from the interior of one side-door Pullman, vigorously and courteously assisted by some brakemen and stockmen with prod poles and chunks of coal." In other words, railroad crew members found some hoboes in a freight car and unceremoniously tossed them out.

"There were about twenty of these tourists, who had come all the way from California in an empty car with empty stomachs, and claimed that they were en route to Florida to 'pick oranges,' though they probably intended to scatter along through San Antonio, Houston and New Orleans and pick pockets," Bonner wrote.

The hoboes did scatter, only to reappear that evening, one by one, at Albert Cockrell's saloon. The frame building fronted Murphy Street on the south side of the railroad tracks, then the town's main drag. Bartender Abe Anglin, described as a "big, fat…jolly, good-natured fellow," had a robust fire blazing in the stove. His customers, mostly cowboys, busied themselves at billiards and "possibly other innocent pastimes at $1 per pass." Outside a light coating of snow covered the ground.

The hoboes, unable to afford a drink or a turn at the tables, sat on a bench near the fire, content merely to be warm. Well, mostly content. "Every time a gang of cowboys would walk up [to the bar] for drinks," Bonner continued with his tale, "these forlorn looking tourists would gaze longingly at the sparkling beverages, and intuitively swallow, just as though they were enjoying the drinks themselves." The "tourists" may or may not have noticed when one of the cowboys bellied up to the bar for a quiet conversation with the barkeep, who nodded in agreement with whatever had been said.

A short time later, Billy Baxter turned to the hoboes and with a friendly, welcoming smile announced that he would be happy to stand them all a drink. "No second invitation was needed," Bonner wrote. The visitors rushed to the bar, and each of them knocked down a warming toddy, all the better tasting being free.

"Charge that to me," the cowboy said beneficently. But then a problem developed. The barkeep pronounced that this cowboy's tab, which already stood at sixty-four dollars for the month, had gone unpaid too long. Asking to see his bill, the cowboy studied it for a moment before throwing the paper across the counter and suggesting a place where Anglin could place it. At the same time, he moved back among the visiting Californians, who, sensing trouble, had already distanced themselves from the discussion.

When the cowboy suddenly pulled a .45 to underscore his annoyance, the hoboes' eyes got as big as locomotive wheels. At about the same moment, the bartender went for his gun. The big man behind the bar let loose on the deadbeat cowboy with his six-shooter, and Baxter fired back in self-defense, dense white gun smoke filling the air and obscuring the view.

Not knowing that both adversaries were only shooting blanks in a preplanned "little side show," the hoboes stampeded like so many lightning-spooked steers, their ears ringing from all the busted caps. Opting for cold air over hot lead, the out-of-towners ran out the door and straight into a taunt rope that another Alpine conspirator had quietly stretched at ankle level outside the bar. The tripping prank victims piled up on the snow-covered street like cars in a train wreck. As soon as they could untangle themselves, they got up and kept running, oblivious to the roars of laughter coming from the saloon.

The story has a happy ending. As soon as they figured that enough time had passed for things to settle down, the hoboes cautiously returned to the bar to see how many people had been killed. When they saw the bartender and the cowboy standing in perfect health, still laughing hard, the transients knew that they'd been pranked.

Having had their fun, the cowboys bought the hoboes drinks for the rest of the night. Even so, as soon as they could, the hung-over hoboes hopped another eastbound freight and got the heck out of Alpine. "Abe Anglin swears some of these fellows had enough hide peeled off their noses to make a pair of boots," Bonner concluded.

Here's Spit in Your Eye

Wearing a lawman's badge, Everett Townsend had killed men. As a pioneer conservationist, he was a prime mover in the creation of Big Bend National Park, but he was not incapable of having a little fun now and then.

A good example is the friendly feud he had with *Alpine Avalanche* editor Nig Bennett over an unusual self-defense ability attributed to *Phrynsoma cornutum*, far better known in Texas as horny toads. Townsend maintained that these critters spat blood out of their eyes when cornered. Bennett asserted that they did not.

While Townsend had years of experience on his side, having crisscrossed the Big Bend by horse and car, Bennett bought ink by the barrel. In other words, as a newspaper editor, he enjoyed a particularly bully pulpit. No matter. Bennett felt journalistically bound to be fair in his reporting.

Accordingly, in the September 8, 1939 edition of his newspaper, he devoted his page-one column, "Mountain Peeks: Glimpses from the Texas Rockies," to an affidavit supposedly sworn and subscribed to by two women of near impeccable veracity: nuns.

First Bennett set the stage: "It seems that Everett Townsend is the only one who is still hot and bothered about the claim that horned toads spit blood. He is still working diligently to prove, to himself probably, that they really do."

With assistance from his friend Jerry Ratliff of the Sul Ross College faculty, Bennett continued, Everett had "secured from a couple of unsuspecting souls" a statement that they had actually seen a horned toad "commit the act."

Bennett also did a little crawfishing. "We have never said the horned toad does NOT spit blood when excited or angry" merely that "we have never seen one do it."

An old lawman and newspaper editor debated the horned toad's purported ability to spit blood like tobacco juice. *Photo by Mike Cox.*

The signed statement came from Sister Frances (christened Sue Mildred Johnson) and Sister Eloysius (christened Madeline Maria Wagner). Both women had attended summer school at Sul Ross.

"On or about June 17, A.D. 1939, we were out walking with dual purpose of exercising ourselves and giving Shoe Buttons [their dog] her daily constitutional," the meat of their statement began. Suddenly, "Shoe Button…attracted our attention by barking and scampering violently." Turning to see what the matter was, the sisters found their dog "making heroic charges upon some tiny beestie. When we approached we discovered that the battle raging was between Shoe Buttons, as aggressor, and his horned toadship, on the defensive."

The dog, they continued, "would alternately charge and retreat, and his toadship...would alternately do the reverse and ditto." Then Shoe Buttons, "in a burst of fury—more valorous than wise—rushed the toad, but suddenly fell back in the face of a counter charge, and began to give tongue to her griefs, real and imagined."

Rushing to the dog's assistance, to their horror the sisters found its face covered with blood. At first they thought that the dog had mortally injured the toad, but upon closer examination, they realized that the fluid had come from the toad. Spitting and running, the small reptile had succeeded in making its escape.

"Maybe the two good sisters were mistaken," Bennett said of their statement. "Maybe the toad in question had a chew of terbaccy in his cheek and was squirting the juice therefrom."

Despite the sworn testimony of the two nuns, and the belief of syndicated newspaper cartoonist Bob Ripley's popular "Ripley's Believe it or Not" feature, Everett Townsend and Jerry Ratliff, Bennett wrote that he still wasn't convinced. "We demand a demonstration," he concluded.

That would have been easier back then than in the twenty-first century, when the iconic lizard has become a rare sight in Texas. Thanks to human predation (from boys shooting them with BB rifles to people collecting them as pets or to gold-plate as jewelry) coupled with the invasive fire ants' consumption of the native ants that horned toads like to eat, they are a threatened species in Texas. Seeing one in the Big Bend, or in most other areas they used to range, has gone from common to rare.

So who was right, an old lawman-rancher who had spent many a day in wild country in the heyday of the horned toad...or a country newspaper editor?

Improbable as it may seem, the ability to squirt blood collected from the capillaries along its eyelids is indeed a built-in horned toad feature. When threatened, the palm-sized critters can send a stream for up to four feet.

The two nuns (or whoever reduced their statement to writing) may have been guilty of overdramatizing the confrontation between their pet and a much-smaller lizard, but they had no confession to make in regard to prevarication.

Law and Disorder

Bud Newman and His Gang

Bud Newman didn't amount to much as an outlaw, but not for lack of grit. When and where Newman came into the world is yet to be discovered, though there's a small Newman family cemetery in Val Verde County on the desolate eastern cusp of the Big Bend country that supports the theory that his people came from around there.

Frank Gray, author of *Pioneering in Southwest Texas*, first met Newman when the youngster's father brought "little black-eyed" Buddy riding along with him when he visited a horse camp in Edwards County, where Gray worked as a cowboy.

"I never saw a more quiet and teachable little boy than Buddy Newman," he wrote. "He seemed to know nothing but to obey his father. Buddy did not use rough or profane language" and plainly had been "brought up under the kindly, thoughtful care of a dear Christian mother." But when Newman got older, Gray continued, he "some way or somehow drifted into the swift current of disorder and lawlessness which prevailed at that time." While Newman never hit the big time, he clearly had aspirations. And his memory lived on well into the twentieth century at Comstock, where some of his exploits occurred.

The late W.E. McCarson, born in Val Verde County in 1912, told me about Newman during a visit to his Comstock residence in the fall of 1987. McCarson said that he got the bare bones of the outlaw's story firsthand in 1936, when an old man walked into his family's store in Comstock.

"Boy," the oldster began, "you been here very long?" McCarson allowed as how he had been in Comstock for all of his twenty-four years. But that wasn't long enough for him to have been around when three horsebackers robbed a Southern Pacific passenger train and then galloped off after some lively shooting. While all of the busted caps left ears ringing, no one got hurt. The old man proceeded to fill McCarson in on the robbery. The reason he knew so many details is because he had been one of the robbers. "They sent me to the pen for it," the store visitor declared, his bitterness as plain as his gray hair.

Four decades after the fact, the ex-con blamed bad whiskey and worse company for his fall. Mainly, it was the robust confidence and lack of judgment associated with overindulgence in spirituous beverages that led to his troubles.

"Those bastards talked me into it," he told McCarson. Among those of alleged doubtful parentage he referred to was Bud Newman.

These days, an investigator can reopen a cold case with a few clicks on a computer keyboard, calling up a suspect's criminal history and other pertinent bits of information. But law enforcement didn't keep such good records in the 1890s. Fortunately for history, newspapers seldom ignore a good story.

Newman first came to the attention of the Texas press late in 1895 when the *Dallas Morning News* reported that on December 1 a "difficulty" between Newman and Shepard Baker ended "after several shots were fired." Newman went to jail and Baker to the cemetery. "Both were young men in the stock business," the newspaper's correspondent added.

McCarson said that the two cowboys shot it out near Kelly's Saloon, conveniently located on a hill overlooking the Comstock bone yard.

The way McCarson heard the story, Newman and Baker had been feuding over some issue long since forgotten. The day of the shooting, Baker happened to be sitting in a wagon when he spotted Newman and promptly took a shot at him. The report of the weapon spooked the team pulling the wagon, and Baker could not get off a second shot. Newman, however, rested his Winchester on the saddle of his borrowed horse and put a round right between Baker's eyes.

Having waived an examining trial, Newman eventually gained release from the county jail in Del Rio on $3,000 bond. Though it escaped the attention of at least the Dallas newspaper, Newman apparently won acquittal in the killing, probably on the grounds of self-defense.

A little more than a year after the Comstock shooting, newspapers readers learned that westbound SP passenger train no. 20 had been robbed at about midnight on December 20, 1896, near Cow Creek less than a mile west of Comstock.

After gaining everyone's attention with the firing of numerous pistol rounds, three men tied up the train crew and took about seventy dollars from what railroad express officials referred to as a "local" safe. The robbers had been unable to open a larger transcontinental safe equipped with a timer lock.

The robbers rode off "to the hills," and the train continued its run. As soon as word of the holdup reached the sheriff, he formed a posse and took up the trail. The next day, several Texas Rangers also rode out in search of the outlaws.

Thanks to ranger Thalis Cook, an expert tracker, the state lawmen made short work of the case. By December 27, they had four men in custody: Newman, Frank Gobble, Alex Purviance and Rollie Shackleford.

Justice moved quickly in those days. The following March, Purviance, described as in "a dying condition with consumption [tuberculosis]," entered a plea of guilty and got five years. A month later, Shackleford also copped a plea for five years. What happened to Gobble's case seems not to have made the public prints, but on October 26, 1897, Newman was acquitted.

Having beaten the rap twice, Newman apparently saw no need to reform. But his good fortune would not hold the next time he got into trouble.

Why Bill Taylor Disappeared

Outlaw Bud Newman apparently believed himself to be bulletproof, figuratively and even literally. After all, he had beaten the rap after killing a man in a gun battle in 1895 and then was acquitted of robbing a Southern Pacific train near Comstock two years later. Not only had Newman come off scot-free, he had made a few bucks for his effort as well.

Evidently, the twenty-three-year-old Newman believed that he could do better. Not better as in going straight, but better in terms of making a bigger score.

At about 11:00 p.m. on June 9, 1898, at a point called Coleman Switch about four miles west of Santa Anna, Newman and three other masked men descended on a Santa Fe passenger train that had stopped there to switch tracks on its run from Brownwood to San Angelo. The other three robbers were later identified as Pierce Keaton and Bill and Jeff Taylor, brothers.

After getting the drop on the train's engineer, some of the gunmen escorted the engineer and fireman Lee Johnson to the always-locked express car and told Johnson to have the messenger open up. Staring into a gun barrel, the fireman did as told. Newman and company planned to blast open the money safe with dynamite once the messenger let them inside.

Unfortunately for the fireman and the robbers, an armed Santa Fe livestock agent riding in one of the passenger cars snapped to the robbery attempt and alighted from the train with a .45 blazing. A general firefight erupted. Johnson crumpled with a gut shot that would prove fatal. Newman took a slug in his right arm, while a bone-shattering ball thudded into Keaton's right leg.

Sans money and in pain, the robbers mounted their horses with varying degrees of ease and galloped off into the night. They pretty much kept riding until they reached Sutton County, 125 miles to the southwest. That's where the Taylor family had a ranch. Meanwhile, back at the crime scene, the train crew put the wounded fireman on board and backed into Santa Anna. A day later, Johnson died.

Lawmen from all over that part of west Texas rushed to Coleman County. Fortunately for investigators, in their haste to escape the would-be robbers had left behind their dynamite. While fingerprint technology had not yet become a forensic tool, the packages containing the explosives bore advertisements from merchants in San Angelo and Sonora. On top of that, the tracks left behind by the fleeing bandits lay in the direction of Sutton County.

Tom Green County sheriff Gerome Shield telephoned the Sutton County sheriff and asked him to see if the retailer in Sonora remembered who he sold the dynamite to. Before long the Sonora lawman had a name. Led by Shield and a deputy U.S. marshal, a multi-agency posse soon headed toward the Taylor Ranch. Without much trouble, the officers arrested Newman and his colleagues.

Apparently figuring that he could game the system one more time, Newman later agreed to flip for the state in exchange for immunity. On his damning testimony, Keaton and Jeff Taylor got ninety-nine years for the murder of the fireman and another eight for the attempted robbery—more years by far than either had to spare.

Bill Taylor got convicted of participating in the botched holdup. But while awaiting trial on the murder charge, he managed to escape from the Coleman County Jail.

Knowing that Taylor would be getting in touch with the now-free Newman, officers got Newman to convince Taylor that he had in mind another train robbery back in Comstock. Taylor fell for it and soon found himself back in the pokey. Finally, it dawned on Taylor that Newman had betrayed him not once but twice. More than a little annoyed, Taylor vowed revenge.

With that mission in mind, Taylor sawed his way out of his cell and made good his escape. Regrettably for him, the first house he came to after fleeing the lockup belonged to the sheriff. Having been taken to a presumably sturdier jail, the Brown County lockup, Taylor broke out a third time in June 1900. Again, the Coleman County sheriff recruited Newman to help him catch Taylor. A posse including Newman caught up with Taylor some seventy miles south of Sonora.

According to a story filed by the Coleman correspondent for the *Dallas Morning News* on August 14, 1900, at some point "Taylor got the drop on Newman and killed him, but not before Newman had fired his Winchester, which took effect in Taylor's groin."

Returned to Brownwood, Taylor said that in killing Newman he had realized "the only object in his life." Now, he allowed, he stood "perfectly willing for the law to take its course." That noble sentiment aside, he soon escaped a fourth time, never to be heard from again. Some said that he crossed the Rio Grande into Mexico. Maybe he went to the Big Bend, an easy place to hide. No matter where he ended up, Bill Taylor had proven that Bud Newman wasn't bulletproof.

"Harry, Don't Kill Me!"

With thousands of U.S. Army horse soldiers already stationed across the Big Bend, and a quarter million National Guardsmen on their way to the border to guard against bandit raids, Alpine may have been one of the safest cities in Texas in the summer of 1916.

A few months earlier, more than one hundred miles to the south, Mexican raiders had attacked the small community of Glenn Springs. That, as well as other incidents spawned by the ongoing Mexican Revolution, had fueled the military buildup. But when gunfire broke out in Alpine on the evening of July 20, the shots did not come from hostile riders who had splashed across the Rio Grande.

Though many residents recognized the sound of pistol fire, those who happened to be closer to the scene heard something else: a woman screaming, "Harry, don't kill me!"

When the shooting stopped, people rushing in the direction of the reports found a Hupmobile crashed into a wire fence in a residential area only a few blocks from the Holland Hotel. Two blood-covered bodies—an attractive young woman and an older man wearing the light tan cotton uniform of a U.S. cavalry officer—lay slumped on the black leather backseat of the touring car.

The dead woman was Crystal Holland Spannell, twenty-nine-year-old daughter of Mr. and Mrs. John R. Holland, owners of Alpine's largest and most popular hotel. Next to her lay Lieutenant Colonel Matthew C. Butler, the fifty-two-year-old commander of the First Squadron of the Sixth U.S. Cavalry.

As bystanders continued to gawk at the gory scene, Harry Johnson Spannell staggered up to the county jail outside the Brewster County Courthouse. When Constable W.J. Yates arrived moments later, he found

Soldiers sent to the Big Bend during the bandit troubles enjoyed the scenery in more ways than one, but in one instance socializing with a local lady led to a double killing.

Spannell crying. As the lawman approached, Spannell asked if they were "both dead." When Yates said yes, Spannell blurted out, "Oh, my God!" Yates asked why he had shot his wife and the army officer. Spannell replied that he did not know. After checking to see if he was armed, the officer led him inside the lockup and placed him in a cell.

For such a large county, Brewster County sheriff J. Allen Walton had only a small force, and Alpine's only lawman was Constable Yates. While Walton and Yates rounded up and interviewed witnesses, a deputy drove Spannell to Marfa to protect against the possibility that family and friends of Mrs. Spannell, or soldiers seeking to revenge the death of a popular officer, might try to string him up.

The next day, a wire service report on the shooting appeared on the front pages of newspapers across the nation. Correctly noting that "mystery surrounds the motive," the story offered a summary of the event that would change in only one respect over a series of trials that dragged on for the next three and a half years:

> *Spannel was driving his wife and Colonel Butler in his car along the main residential street…when suddenly Spannell stopped the car, turned in his seat, drew an automatic* [semiautomatic] *pistol and a revolver and with the one began shooting Colonel Butler and with the other his wife. After emptying both weapons he got out of the car, walked to the Courthouse and gave himself up.*

While the county attorney collected evidence to present to the grand jury, the army quickly dispatched a colonel to Alpine to investigate Butler's death. But even before that officer issued his report, the ranking officer at the cavalry camp near Alpine, Colonel J.E. Muchert, labeled it a "cold-blooded, premeditated murder, committed by a man crazed with jealousy."

Indeed, no one could come up with any proof that Butler had ever conducted himself improperly with Mrs. Spannell. The army's official report, released July 25, supported that.

By September, Spannell had been indicted on two counts of murder. Later that month, District Judge Joe Jones granted a defense motion for a change of venue, ordering that Spannell be tried in San Angelo for his wife's murder.

The trial began on January 16, 1917, and continued through February 2. The state sought the death penalty, but the twelve-man jury saw it differently

Crystal Holland's grave in Alpine. *Photo by Mike Cox.*

and found Spannell not guilty. His defense attorneys had managed to convince the jury that he had only accidentally shot his wife, no matter that she had been heard pleading with him not to kill her.

Bowed but not beaten, the state then prosecuted Spannell for Butler's death. That trial, held in Coleman, resulted in Spannell's conviction on May 5 and a five-year prison sentence. His lawyers filed an appeal and got the case remanded to district court for another trial. This time the trial would be in Brownwood, in the same judicial district as Coleman.

When Spannell, who had been free on $5,000 bond, and his lawyer drove into Brownwood from Waco, the counselor's briefcase fat with depositions he had collected in Waco and Mission, where Butler had been stationed before being ordered to the Big Bend. The depositions from Waco were signed by people who swore that Spannell was a fine family man; the depositions from Mission came from people asserting that Butler had the reputation of being "a libertine, a woman chaser and a man seeking illicit relations with women."

Jury selection began January 5, but by the end of the day only seven had been picked. The judge had to call for another venue, finally getting a full jury empanelled on January 7. The state took the rest of the week to present its case, essentially the same testimony produced in the two previous trials. Spannell's legal team started its defense on January 13. All of the glowing depositions regarding Spannell got admitted to evidence, as did the statements from the Rio Grande Valley disparaging Colonel Butler's character.

The case went to the jury on January 18, and that afternoon the jury returned its verdict: innocent. Any chance of Spannell being punished for the death of his wife and that of Colonel Butler had ended. He may finally have been a free man, but Spannell told Brown County sheriff R.B. Pugh that he was not all that eager to leave the confines of his cell. In fact, if the sheriff didn't mind, he'd just as soon stay locked up until the next morning, when he planned to leave town.

That was fine with Pugh. As the local newspaper put it, the sheriff agreed to let Spannell spend one more night on Brown County's nickel "to avoid possible disturbances on the streets, where there was considerable feeling following the announcement of the jury's verdict." In other words, the sheriff wasn't so sure that some of his constituents might not decide that Spannell needed hanging despite his acquittal. At 7:30 a.m. the following morning, Spannell quietly left the jail for Waco. There, he planned to pass a few days with some of his friends before leaving for his father's residence in Hazelton, Pennsylvania.

Spannell stayed in his home state for nearly two decades, returning to Texas and settling in Waco in 1939. Unlike the two people he had been acquitted of shooting to death so many years before, he made it to nearly seventy, dying on October 2, 1947, following a heart attack. He's buried at Oakwood Cemetery there.

Though he figured in scores of newspaper stories from the time of the murders until the day before his departure from Brownwood on January 19, 1920, Harry Spannell died in obscurity, the passions that ruled his life as a younger man long gone.

Harvey Hughes's Short Literary Career

Like most elected officials, Brewster County sheriff E.E. Townsend received a fair amount of correspondence, from postcards bearing descriptions of wanted felons to legal papers to magazines, but the package that arrived from San Antonio that day in March 1923 ranked as the most unusual piece of mail he ever received.

Though he knew what it contained, the lawman couldn't help but open the box right away. Inside, coiled like a skinny, hairy rattlesnake, lay a length of rope. Townsend could have gone to any of several stores in town and used county funds to buy a rope, but in this case he preferred woven hemp that had seen some use. When it came time for his prisoner to hang, the former Texas Ranger wanted the young man in his custody to die quickly. To that end, his friend Bexar County sheriff John W. Tobin had assured him that this rope had done its work of breaking the neck of the late Clemente Apolinar, a convicted killer, quite effectively. Tobin didn't even want the rope returned, since a law would soon go into effect transferring the responsibility of capital punishment to the Texas prison system, where future executions would be in an electric chair.

Being on the mainline of the Southern Pacific Railroad ensured modest growth and prosperity for Alpine, but sometimes it brought trouble, which is why Townsend needed the rope.

When a long westbound freight train rumbled to a stop at Alpine on the night of January 24, 1922, a brakeman heard what sounded like groaning coming from one of the boxcars. Calling for help, he slid open the door and shined his lantern inside. The light revealed the prostrate form of a semiconscious man with a handkerchief tied over his mouth as a gag.

With help from local law enforcement officers, the brakeman got the man out of the freight car and laid him on a cot in a nearby work train that had living quarters for railroad men. The doctor summoned to examine the man found that he had been shot in the back, the projectile having pierced his liver and lungs. On top of that, he had been beaten.

Lucid for a time, the young man described the person he had been traveling with and summarized what had happened to him by declaring that it was "hell to feed a man and then have him shoot you in the back for $20." All the doctor could do for the moribund young man was give him a shot for his pain and stay with him until he died, which happened at 2:30 a.m. the following day.

Later that morning at Toronto, six miles west of Alpine, Deputy Sheriff Tom Morgan found a transient matching the description the victim had given of his assailant. Identified as Harvey Hughes, the twenty-one-year-old also had property believed to have belonged to the murdered man: a fountain pen, a watch and some money.

After that, the criminal justice system moved quickly. Not even a month after the murder, a Brewster County jury found Hughes guilty and assessed his punishment as death. Hughes's attorney then asked for a sanity hearing for his client, a motion the judge granted. On March 3, 1923, a jury found Hughes sane on the same day the Texas Court of Criminal Appeals turned down a motion for a new trial.

In early April, just in time to get a brief story on page five of that week's edition of the *Alpine Avalanche*, the editor learned of the telegram that Sheriff Townsend had received that morning from Governor Pat Neff: "This is to advise you that it is not my intention to interfere in any way with the verdict of the jury and the judgment of the court in Harvey Hughes case." In other words, the young Ohio man would hang for murder.

"A scaffold is being erected on the north side of the courthouse from which the unfortunate young man will be hanged, unless of course, Gov. Neff changes his mind," the newspaper speculated. "The hanging will be private—only the necessary attendants will be present. The execution will take place Saturday—the first vindication of the law against murder in Brewster County."

That was a polite way of saying that Hughes's execution would be the first ever legal hanging in Texas's largest political subdivision. In fact, it would be the only official execution anywhere in the Big Bend and one of the last in the state's history. (The final judicially sanctioned hanging occurred in Brazoria County, in southeast Texas, on August 31 that year.)

While the story the newspaper published that day ran only three paragraphs, the description of Hughes as "the unfortunate young man" was telling. For a convicted killer, Hughes seems to have become fairly well thought of, despite his short-lived escape from jail the previous October 15. In March 1923, the governor had received a petition signed by numerous Alpine residents asking that he commute Hughes's sentence to life in prison.

Now that it seemed certain that he would die, Hughes began a late-in-life literary career, writing a surprisingly cogent mini-memoir. He said that it was the first thing he had ever written. "I have been what you might call an habitual criminal," he wrote. "And I thought I was getting happiness and everything that goes with it, but was very badly mistaken. I have known about every type of crook on the face of the earth, and I am sorry to say it…I can not begin to say how sorry I am, for taking a human life, a very much valued human treasure."

On Saturday, April 7, as Hughes stood on the gallows listening to the preacher's prayer, he received a final courtesy from Sheriff Townsend. To spare his prisoner from having to know the exact moment of his death, the sheriff sprang the trap in mid-prayer before the young man expected it.

The previously used rope did its work, snapping Hughes's neck. Fifteen minutes later, at noon, Dr. M.L. Turney pronounced him dead. Later that afternoon, as workmen tore down the gallows, a county crew buried Hughes in Alpine's city cemetery.

The Lady in Chartreuse

The burning greasewood fire made a small orange glow against the night sky. The briefly flickering flame was the funeral pyre of a woman whose bones were later found scattered on a rocky hillside three and a half miles from the Brewster County town of Lajitas. If there were any mourners, no one knows, because no one even knows who the woman was. For Carl Williams, who served for five years as sheriff of the sprawling county, the woman remains the "Lady in Chartreuse."

Two men found human skeletal remains near an old candelilla wax vat on July 29, 1965, a scorching summer day. Ramon and Chon Amendariz told officers that they had stumbled across the bones by accident. They said, however, that they had seen some unusual buzzard activity in the area some three weeks earlier.

An initial wire service story reflects the insensitive language of the day:

> *"Wet Back" Finds Body of Woman*
> *United Press International*
> *Alpine, Tex., July 30.—State highway patrolman Jean Pate said today that the badly burned body of a 20–34 year-old white woman found near the Rio Grande 90 miles south of here apparently had been there about a month. Pate said that a Mexican laborer had come across the body yesterday afternoon in desolate brush country about 1½ miles east of Ranch Road 170 and about 3 miles from the hamlet of Lajitas, just west of Big Bend National Park. Pate said there was some indication the woman had been in a sleeping bag and that someone had thrown gasoline over the bag and set it afire.*

Sheriff Williams and Alpine-based Texas Ranger Arthur Hill reached the scene later in the day. The bones had been scattered and chewed on by animals, but remnants of cloth lay where the body had been burned. A gasoline can had been discarded nearby. The officers also found tracks that appeared to have been left by a pickup truck that led a mile and a half from Texas 170 to the hill where the body had been burned, but they turned up nothing else that appeared to be connected to the case.

The following day, the two lawmen and others began a fruitless three-day ground and aerial search of the desolate area. With help from the Brewster County Rescue Squad, they found a few more bones, but that was it.

Hill drove the remains to Austin for analysis at the Texas Department of Public Safety crime lab. The report indicated that the bones were those of a Caucasian woman, between thirty and forty years old, five feet, five inches tall, with light brown and partially gray hair. Studying the remnants of the woman's clothing, DPS forensic specialists concluded that she had been wearing a light chartreuse shirt-type blouse, green knit stretch pants and a light reversible jacket.

All of the woman's left ribs had been broken or had cracked. A dental expert

A doll dressed like the Lady in Chartreuse. *Photo by Mike Cox.*

who examined the skull said that the woman had never had any work done before her death, thus ruling out any possibility of identifying her through dental records. A .38-caliber lubloid slug had been found near the bones, but the lab examination was not conclusive that a gunshot wound had been the cause of death, though there was a hole in one of the woman's scapula.

The investigators checked numerous missing person reports, but in each case something prevented a name from being matched with the remains. By the time he left office on December 31, 1969, Williams's case file bulged with reports of women who had disappeared, but none of them accurately fit the description of the "Lady in Chartreuse."

About two months after the discovery of the skeleton, another mystery turned up: a crude wooden cross at the site of the cremation. Nails driven into the wood formed this legend: "Cadeb Encontro Este Julio 29 de 1965 se." (Corpse found here, July 29, 1965.)

"The cross appeared on the hill sometime during the span of two months," Williams recalled. "I'd go back down there from time to time, thinking whoever put the body there might return. There was a span of about two months I didn't go down there. I guess it was put there about that time."

Shortly after the discovery, Ranger Hill purchased a small doll and had a local seamstress sew some doll clothes patterned after the garments found near Lajitas. The DPS circulated pictures of the doll to law enforcement agencies across the state and nation.

"If we could ever find anyone who could make positive identification of the remains we'd have a lot more to go on," Williams said in a 1969 newspaper interview. "It's pretty hard to solve a murder when you don't even know who got killed."

It developed that the death probably wasn't a murder after all, though there's still a mystery involved. What follows is the rest of the story.

Now retired from law enforcement, Williams spent countless man-hours on the case before he left office. Eventually, the sheriff and Ranger Hill focused on the registered owner of a pickup truck who had been seen pulling a camper trailer in Big Bend National Park. Before the discovery of the body, Highway Patrolman Pate had investigated an accident in which a trailer had come loose from a vehicle and rolled down a steep slope. The accident appeared to have been routine, but the officers later learned that the driver of the vehicle, a traveling piano tuner who periodically visited the Big Bend, had been traveling with a woman who was not his wife. They believed that when the trailer rolled, that woman had been inside and was

Brewster County sheriff Carl Williams indicating the spot where bones were found in 1965. *Photo by Mike Cox.*

killed. Panicking, the driver dragged his dead paramour from the wreckage of the camper, drove to the point where the Lady in Chartreuse was later found and burned the body to avoid any embarrassing revelations.

"We were pretty sure that's what happened," Williams said years later, "but we never developed enough evidence to prove it in court. The big problem was that we were never able to learn who the woman was. If we could have identified her, I believe we could have tied her to the suspect and made a case, even though if it happened like we think it did, it wouldn't have been homicide."

Characters

The Hunchback of Ojinaga

He had a given name, but along the Rio Grande in the vicinity of Presidio, people mostly called him the hunchback, or the hunchback bandit.

Despite the medical condition that gave him a notably curved spine, this man did not lack backbone in the figurative sense. Skilled with six-gun or rifle and passionate in his beliefs, the hunchback first came to the attention of authorities in Mexico and Texas in the early 1890s when he rode as a lieutenant with a band of revolution-minded Chihuahuans inspired by Teresa Urrea, a charismatic *curandera* better known along the border as Santa Teresa or La Santa de Cabora.

For the hunchback, what began as armed participation in a political movement laced with mysticism degenerated into banditry on both sides of the border as the Santa Teresa movement faltered against ruthless federal resistance. But his association with Urrea left him believing in the accessibility of a mystical power that could not only cure the afflicted but also protect one from harm.

At the time, former Texas Ranger E.E. Townsend worked as a customs inspector stationed in Presidio. Part of his job involved collecting duties on the large herds of cattle then coming into Texas from Mexico. Usually, the vaquero in charge of a herd paid in coin—silver U.S. money. Townsend sometimes had responsibility for thousands of dollars in silver. To start the money on its long journey from the Big Bend to Washington, Townsend would take it from Presidio to the stagecoach office at Shafter, then a thriving mining town, and send it off in a U.S. mailbag.

Following an extraordinary run of cattle shipments from Mexico to Texas, Townsend got word from a friend in Mexico that the hunchback and his gang intended to waylay the federal officer and relieve him of all of the silver that he had collected in duties. Expecting the worst, Townsend suggested that his wife head for Marfa until the trouble could be handled, but she refused to leave.

The day before the stage's regularly scheduled arrival at Shafter, Townsend saddled his horse and leisurely rode out of Presidio for what folks logically assumed to be one of his periodic scouts along the river in search of smugglers. People could tell that he wasn't going to Shafter or he would have headed north on the Shafter Road. Even the fact that he held his Winchester across the saddle was not unusual.

Keeping his horse to a trot, Townsend moved east of town along the river, slowly angling to the northeast. Anyone watching him would have been able to tell that he wasn't in a hurry to get anywhere.

Of course, the federal officer was indeed slowly working his way to Shafter. The leather morral tied to his saddle, a large feedbag he always carried, held the oats he always carried. But beneath the horse feed rested nearly $7,000 in silver, a small fortune back then.

A man carrying that much money normally would ride fast, nervous about being ambushed and robbed. But Townsend stuck to a slow pace so as not to attract attention. Also, he wanted to be able to hear the clatter of horse hooves if anyone started following him.

Finally, Townsend rode into the busy little town of Shafter to meet the incoming stage and get the silver on its way to safety. His effort to thwart the hunchback's planned holdup had worked perfectly.

Safely back in Presidio, Townsend soon learned from his network of informants that the hunchback had abandoned his robbery plans in favor of more pressing business: avoiding capture by federal authorities in his own country. The Santa Teresa movement had continued to fade, and most of the hunchback's followers no longer followed. In fact, only five men had stayed with him.

Not long after the customs inspector had to take extra measures to ensure the safe shipment of the duties he had collected, Townsend got word that Mexican soldiers had the hunchback and his men cornered in a small adobe building on the edge of Ojinaga. Even so, as long as their rifle ammunition held out, the bandits were managing to keep the besieging troops at bay.

On the third day, though outnumbered twenty to one, the hunchback decided to take the offensive. When his men seemed reluctant to join him in abandoning their cover to rush the surrounding ring of uniformed soldiers, the hunchback delivered an inspiring speech. Theirs was a holy war against government oppression, he said. Haranguing them for their lack of faith, he assured his men that they were fighting for the right thing.

The government soldiers, their rifles at the ready, lay near enough to the hunchback's position to hear as he shouted to his men, "Charge your impious foes and when they fire at you just blow their bullets away…as if they were feathers. The bullets cannot harm you."

The hunchback's words inspired his men. As waiting squads of soldiers leveled their rifles and each man worked the bolt to chamber a round, the remaining *Teresitas* burst forth from their adobe cover, their lips pursed to blow away like so many butterflies any bullets that might fly their way. Unfortunately for the revolution-minded outlaws, assuming that they had any time to think, they quickly discovered that, contrary to what they had been assured, puffs of air did not stop bullets.

In time, revolution did come to northern Mexico, and the long reign of President Porfirio Díaz ended, but the hunchback and his followers were not around to see it.

Elmo Johnson

The outbreak of the Mexican Revolution in 1910 brought bandit raids and periodic violence that continued well into the 1920s in the Big Bend. Though he entered the picture near the end of this turbulent period, a man named Elmo Johnson relied on his reputed shooting abilities to stay safe. Of course, he had a little help from the army.

In the fall of 1967, then a young reporter for the *San Angelo Standard-Times*, I drove to Sonora to interview Johnson. He lived on his family's ranch in a little house on the edge of town. I don't remember whether it was my idea to visit him or just another assignment from my editor, but I'm sure glad that I talked to him. As best as I can tell all these years later, I'm the only person who ever asked him questions and took notes on what he had to say. My only regret is that I didn't pump him harder for stories about his days along the Rio Grande.

An aerial view of Johnson's Trading Post.

Johnson, seventy-nine when I met him, had been living in Sonora since 1945. For a time, he had operated a sporting goods store there, but by the mid-1960s he had retired, spending most of his time gardening and feeding deer and turkey on his ranch. But I wasn't much interested in what Johnson had to say about his place in Sonora. I wanted to talk to him about his time in the Big Bend, when he operated a river-crossing trading post sixteen miles downstream from Castolon in the part of the Big Bend called the "Big Loop."

He and his wife, Ada, had gone there in late 1926, only eight years after the last of the bandit raids connected to the Mexican Revolution, long before the area had any paved roads and nearly two decades before the Big Bend National Park was opened.

Born in Fannin County in 1889, Johnson and his family moved to Dallas when he was fourteen. After he got out of school, he worked for Dunn and Bradstreet for a time before deciding in 1910 to settle on two sections of family land in Sutton County. In 1918, he got drafted, but by the time he reported for processing in San Antonio, the armistice had been signed. Having sold his west Texas land, he decided to stay in the Alamo City and go into the house-building business. He built several blocks of homes but didn't think that he was making enough money and sold out. That's when he and his wife decided to come to the Big Bend.

Trading a ranch he owned in Kendall County, Johnson acquired just shy of a thousand acres in Brewster County from G.N. Graddy, a Kentuckian who had tried raising everything from tobacco to watermelons on the rich

Rio Grande floodplain fronting the property. On the flat above he had built an eighty- by forty-foot adobe building with commercial space on one end, a master living area on the other end and several smaller rooms in between. The building also featured a large, roofed, screened-in porch with a view of the river. Across that river lay a small Mexican village.

Johnson planned to operate a trading post and grow cotton, but the pink boll worm took care of the cotton growing idea. Agriculturally, he had his best success growing vegetables to sell at his store, but before long, tourists became his best cash crop. Central to attracting visitors was selling the idea that despite its extreme isolation and proximity to Mexico, his ranch was a safe place to spend time fishing or swimming in the river or simply relaxing and enjoying the wonderful scenery.

Boasting that he could knock the eye of out a jackrabbit with his pistol at fifty yards, and that people along both sides of his part of the river knew that, Johnson never locked his business. "I didn't have to," he said, "because I kept the peace. We never had as much as a watermelon stolen."

One example of his peacekeeping came shortly after he and his wife moved to the river. Johnson tried to make a citizen's arrest of a man he believed to be a fugitive. "I chased him in my car until I couldn't go any farther," he recalled. "He got off his horse and started running, and I let him go. He went to the sheriff in Alpine and said he wanted to file charges on me for shooting at him."

The sheriff, a deputy and two Texas Rangers showed up at the trading post the next day. Guided to the scene of the confrontation, the lawmen couldn't find any empty shell casings.

Johnson was not around at the time but went to the sheriff's office as soon as he heard that the lawmen had been looking into the incident. As the trading post proprietor explained that he had only chased the man, not shot at him three times as he had claimed, a ranger who knew him spoke up in his behalf.

"Elmo, I told 'em it was a damn lie," he said. "You wouldn't have shot but once, anyway." Nothing further came of the matter.

All went well until April 11, 1929, when thirty Mexican bandits struck the ranch, driving off all of Johnson's livestock. The army dispatched a troop of cavalry to guard the trading post and patrol the river from there, but airplanes could cover a lot more territory than horses.

"I talked the air corps into putting in a landing strip at my ranch near the trading post," he said. "Back in those days, there was no night flying, and my place was a good location for a stopover."

Elmo Johnson feeds wild turkeys on his ranch near Sonora in 1967. *Photo by Mike Cox.*

The army also put in a radio station at the ranch, and Johnson became an unpaid operative for army intelligence, G-2. Johnson used the radio, which had one soldier assigned as its operator, to report any suspicious activity along his part of the river.

Military aviators and army brass who pulled rank to hitch rides in planes considered the trading post as much a resort as a landing field. Among the notable military visitors were General Jonathan M. Wainwright, destined for fame during World War II at Corregidor, and Major Nathan F. Twining, future chairman of the Joint Chiefs of Staff. Well-known civilian guests over the years included novelist John Dos Passos, sculptor Gutzon Borglum, aviatrix Amelia Earhart and historian Walter Prescott Webb.

The airfield was shut down in 1943. The National Park was opened a year later. A year after that, having sold their property to the government for inclusion in the park, the Johnsons said goodbye to the Big Bend and moved to Sonora.

Ada died of cancer at fifty-four in 1945. Johnson lived out the rest of his life on his ranch. In 1974, not long after a final visit to the Big Bend to see the ruins of his old trading post, he suffered a stroke and died on Christmas Eve.

Three Big Bend Women

The Queen of the Pecos

Almost everyone has heard of Pecos Bill, the mythical west Texas cowboy, but the "fair young" Pecos River Queen never got the attention she deserves. Her name, according to a century-old cowboy poem that commemorates her, was Patty Moorehead.

First some background. In 1892, about a decade after the Southern Pacific laid its tracks through west Texas, the railroad considerably shortened the route by building a huge bridge across the lower Pecos. That river—Texas's westernmost if you don't count the Rio Grande—winds like a rattlesnake across west Texas, emptying into Lake Amistad.

An engineering marvel, the Pecos River Viaduct (as it was formally known) spanned 2,180 feet and towered 321 feet above the river. For years the metal structure ranked as the highest bridge in the United States and the third highest in the world. Postcards of the bridge, the eastern gateway to the Big Bend, became a favorite medium for the classic "Having a good time, wish you were here" message.

Gutsy local cowboys, confident that they had a good horse and perhaps further emboldened by a little whiskey, occasionally rode across the walkway that adjoined the tracks on the bridge. There were no guardrails.

Naturally, any cowpoke who could walk his horse across a bridge taller than a thirty-two-story building earned quite a reputation. Such a fellow

A cowboy rode his horse across this bridge to win the heart of the Pecos River Queen.

would be a suitable partner for the Pecos River Queen, a gal as handy at throwing a loop as she was pretty. The poem, long in public domain, begins as follows:

Where the Pecos River winds and turns in its journey to the sea,
From its white walls of sand and rock striving ever to be free,
Near the highest railroad bridge that all these modern times have seen
Dwells fair young Patty Moorhead, the Pecos River Queen.
She's known by all the cowboys on the Pecos River wide;
They know full well that she can shoot, that she can rope and ride;
She goes to every round-up, every cow-work without fail,
Looking out for all her cattle branded "walking hog on a rail."
She made her start in cattle, yes, made it with her rope;
Can tie down e'ry maverick 'fore it can strike a lope;
She can rope and tie and brand it as quick as any man;
She's voted by all cowboys an A-1 top cow-hand.

N. Howard "Jack" Thorp composed the poem in New Mexico in June 1901. Including it in a book of poetry published seven years later, he noted, "Written on Lower Pecos...after Roy Bean had told me of this fact concerning Patty."

Thorp, a blue-blooded New Yorker who came west at nineteen after a decline in his family's financial health, was referring to the infamous Judge Roy Bean, the "Law West of the Pecos." In truth, Bean was just a boozy eccentric who made good newspaper and magazine copy.

Whether Patty was a fictional character dreamed up by Thorp has not been proven or disproven, but there's some evidence that she was real. The 1900 Del Rio phone book does show a J.R. Moorehead as a cattle rancher living in Comstock. Patty might have been his daughter. And National Park Service historians found that a Patty Moorehead Wilkins leased out some ranch land near the Pecos High Bridge in the 1920s.

Thorp's resume, however, is readily available. Born in New York in 1867, he came to New Mexico in 1886. An accomplished polo player and horse trainer, he took to cowboying. He also did some civil engineering, but the infrastructure he preferred was a good saddle.

In 1898, he pushed a herd from the territory to Higgins, in the Texas Panhandle. Along the way, he wrote a poem called "Little Joe, the Wrangler." It became a cowboy classic and was later recorded to music.

Having an eastern prep school education plus three years at Harvard, Thorp was smart enough to realize that the cowboy songs and poems he heard around the campfire needed to be saved for posterity. He wrote them down, added poems and songs of his own (including "The Pecos Queen") and published them in *Songs of the Cowboys* in 1908. An expanded version of his book, with an introduction by Alice Corbin Henderson, came out in 1921. It had more of his original material.

"'Jack' Thorp…is the genuine thing," Henderson wrote. "He is an old-time cattleman and cowpuncher, and his songs are the fruit of experience. His gift is instinctive and naive, like that of all real cowboy poets, and its charm is precisely in its fresh and 'unliterary' quality."

The last verse of Thorp's poem tells the rest of Patty's story:

Across the Comstock railroad bridge, the highest in the West,
Patty rode her horse one day a lover's heart to test;
For he told her he would gladly risk all dangers for her sake,
But the puncher wouldn't follow, so she's still without a mate.

The old bridge is gone, replaced by a more modern span, but the poem about Patty endures. And if the Patty in the poem was Patty Moorehead Wilkins, she apparently did finally find a fellow who measured up to her standards.

Lizzie Closson

Lizzie Closson had true grit.

Born and raised in New Orleans, Lizzie married George Closson at Brenham in 1866. The couple moved to San Antonio, but Closson spent much of his time well beyond the frontier as a freighter hauling goods to Santa Fe, as well as across the Big Bend to Mexico along the Chihuahua Trail. Closson made a good living, but he had to keep his wife and children in San Antonio.

First as a teamster, later as a wagon train captain and finally as the owner of a freighting business, Closson traveled a lot of miles across the Southwest. He had been running freight to Fort Davis for years and considered the Davis Mountains to be the best country he'd seen. Acquiring property in Musquiz Canyon in about 1876, he sold hay to the army. In 1878, realizing that it wouldn't be too many years before the railroad came through west Texas and put him out of business, he decided to settle in Presidio County and switch to raising sheep.

Closson bought 60 bucks in central Texas and hauled the sheep west from San Antonio in three wagons. Turning them out on his Musquiz Canyon land, he added 1,800 ewes he had purchased from pioneer Big Bend rancher Milton Faver. Perhaps based on the number of children he had by then, he registered his brand as "5." Now he sent for his wife and family.

George and Lizzie Closson raised sheep in Musquiz Canyon near Fort Davis.

The journey by wagon train from San Antonio to Fort Davis would be dangerous, the more so the farther west the covered freight wagons rolled. While the Comanches had been defeated, the survivors relegated to a reservation in the Indian Territory, the same could not be said for the Apaches. The Mescaleros stubbornly clung to their land and their culture, killing any whites they could.

The trek westward would take about a month, at a pace of twelve to fifteen miles a day. Lizzie, her children and another young woman were the only passengers among the freighters. When the train made camp each evening, before turning the teams out to graze, the wagon master saw that the wagons were arranged in a semicircle in case of Indian attack.

As her friend Bessie Jacobs later wrote, Lizzie brought with her to the Big Bend "the tradition of the East and the Old South, and…in a new country she met every difficulty with her unfailing energy and adaptability, conquering hardships hard to conceive of in this day." Two more tangible items she took along were the family piano and a shotgun. She knew how to use both.

Lizzie proved her mettle early on when she heard that one of the teamsters had become too sick to travel. Rather than delay their trip, the wagon master intended to leave the man by the roadside with food and water. On the surface, that seemed humane, but Lizzie understood the reality: the man would be left to die. Whether by charm or threat, Lizzie prevailed on the wagon master to stop long enough for the man to recover, a process she nursed him through.

When the wagon train finally reached Fort Davis, the remote mountain community threw a dance to welcome the new arrivals. That would have made Lizzie feel right at home, but unfortunately, she didn't have one. Though his sheep now grazed in Musquiz Canyon, Closson had not yet had time to build a house for his family, and no one had a residence in Fort Davis he could buy or rent. Fortunately, the curate of the local Catholic church let the Clossons stay there until they could get a house built.

Closson had experienced some close calls with Indians along the trail, and they still caused him problems. As Carlysle Raht wrote in 1919 in his *Romance of the Davis Mountains*, "The Indians seemed to prefer sheep to cattle, as they could be driven more easily…over mountain passes; and, when pressed closely by irate citizens or soldiers, the Indian herders could secret the sheep in small bunches, where their tracks would pass unnoticed by the trailers."

Indians never harmed any of the Clossons, but when one of their sons didn't show up at home when expected, the couple feared that the child had

In 1884, the Clossons moved to a ranch on Calamity Creek in Brewster County and started raising cattle.

been captured by Apaches. Notified of the disappearance, General Edward Ord, the ranking military officer in Texas, wired Fort Davis's commander to deploy every soldier at the post to look for the missing youngster. It turned out that the boy had merely wandered off and was found unharmed.

The military once had been the only vestige of government in the area, but local government came with the organization of Presidio County. Closson served for a time as a Presidio County commissioner and was also on the school board.

The Clossons stayed in the Fort Davis area until 1884, when they moved to a ranch that they had acquired three years earlier on Calamity Creek south of Alpine. However, two years later, Closson died. Now with six children, Lizzie had a family to raise and a ranch to run. When the sheep business went belly up because of the so-called Cleveland Tariff, a measure that severely affected the wool market, Lizzie and other ranchers in the area turned to cattle.

In 1888, Lizzie filed the requisite paperwork with the federal government to seek restitution for property losses incurred by Indian depredations from 1875 to 1877 and additional raids in 1879–80. The early years represented losses that her husband had experienced while still hauling freight, the later years reflecting theft of their sheep by Mescalero Apaches. The full amount of the claim came to $19,625—a fortune in those days. The U.S. Court of

Claims saw it the same way, ruling that the evidence did not support that large a financial loss. In late 1901, the government finally awarded Mrs. Closson $2,590, less attorney's fees.

"Mrs. Closson met difficult situations in a matter of fact way," her friend later wrote. "Nothing seemed too large or too small for her to do. To drive thirty miles and sleep in a box car on a siding, waiting to flag a train to send her child to college was just part of a day's work."

Lizzie Closson died on November 17, 1924, survived by three sons, two daughters and a reputation for having been one strong lady.

The Lady Shot a Lion

Hallie Crawford Stillwell was the only woman I ever knew who killed a mountain lion. I met her in 1967 as a cub reporter for the *San Angelo Standard-Times*. She was the longtime justice of the peace in Alpine and also the San Angelo newspaper's local correspondent. If you needed to know something about Brewster County, or anywhere else in the Big Bend, you called Hallie Stillwell. Or you read her book, *How Come It's Called That: Place Names in the Big Bend Country*.

We stayed friends long after I left the employ of the San Angelo newspaper, though as she aged, I got locked in her memory as that young reporter from "Angelo." In west Texas, the "San" is understood. Anytime I had a chance when I was in the Big Bend country ("country" is colloquial west Texan for "area," as in the Angelo country), I tried to stop by the Stillwell Ranch south of Marathon to visit with Hallie.

Like many of her generation—men and women who grew up before radio, television and other media made it less necessary to entertain ourselves through conversation—she was a fine storyteller, a trait that has always attracted me to people like a June bug to a porch light. And even though she also was a writer, she didn't mind sharing her stories over coffee. The first story on the first page of my first book—a ghost story—is one I heard from Hallie.

In the spring of 1990, doing research on the western writer Zane Grey and his experience with the Texas Rangers, I called on Hallie for information. A Big Bend resident since her arrival by covered wagon in 1910, Hallie had known two of the old border rangers whom Grey had honored in the dedication of his 1915 novel, *Lone Star Ranger*.

One of those rangers was Joe Sitters, who died not long after Grey's western came out when Mexican bandits ambushed him and several other horseback lawmen in a remote mountain pass in Presidio County. The other ranger Hallie had known was Jefferson Eagle Vaughn, a man who had nearly ended Hallie's life prematurely.

As Hallie later told the story to me, Vaughn had been sweet on her sister. One afternoon, trying to impress her with his prowess as a lawman, with great dramatic flourish Vaughn whipped out his six-shooter. The .45 accidentally discharged, leaving a neat round hole under the chair Hallie happened to be occupying. When the gun smoke cleared, the bloom had sort of faded from the budding romance between Vaughn and her sister.

Until her memory slowly began to wane as the years piled up like so many boulders, Hallie was a one-person reference desk for information on the Big Bend. Her book on Big Bend place names, written with her friend Virginia Madison, was first published in 1958. It was revised and reissued by the same publisher, New York–based October House. Twenty years later, another edition, this one in soft cover, was published. The 131-page book still is one of the best sources of information—and good stories—on the Big Bend.

The author interviewing Hallie Stillwell in 1996. *Photo by Linda Cox.*

For a long time, Hallie was something of a local treasure, not widely known east of the Pecos. But her recognition grew steadily over the years as other writers discovered her. Honors and publicity accumulated. She was a friend of Lady Bird Johnson, former governor Ann Richards and hundreds of plain folks. In 1991, a museum dedicated to Hallie's interesting life was opened at her ranch/RV park/store.

The same year, Texas A&M University Press published her memoir, *I'll Gather My Geese.* The book is the story of a hard life made easier by a good sense of humor. Her husband, Roy, died in a truck crash in 1948, but Hallie managed to keep their ranch running and mother her three children.

When a big mountain lion started poaching deer on their ranch, Hallie saddled up, loaded her .30-.30 and went after it. A bullet between the cat's eyes soon ended its taste for venison.

Hallie also managed to survive a problem she couldn't handle with her lever-action rifle: the terrible drought of the early 1950s. Despite the financial hardships brought on by the record dry spell, she held on to her ranch. She supported her family by doing everything from working in a flower shop to saddling up and working her cattle.

The title of her memoir, which at first glance seems a bit strange for a book on a ranchwoman's life in west Texas, perfectly summed up her personality. The line goes back to 1916, when Hallie announced to her father that she was going to teach school in Presidio. Presidio is across the Rio Grande from Ojinaga, Mexico, which not long before had been captured by General Francisco Villa, far better known as Pancho Villa.

"You're going on a wild goose chase," her father told her.

"Then I'll gather my geese," Hallie snapped.

She took the teaching job, and she kept gathering her own geese right up until her death, which came on August 18, 1997, just shy of her 100th birthday. Her independent spirit and overall strength of character never left her. That's one of the reasons my wife, Linda, and I had named our daughter Hallie three years earlier. (Dadie Stillwell, Hallie's daughter, later told us that we were not the first couple to have that idea. Texas has several younger Hallie's among its citizens, thanks to Hallie Stillwell.)

In addition to the books she wrote, Hallie served as a significant resource for several other writers, including Austin historian Ken Ragsdale. He wrote two Big Bend–related books that benefited from her help and had been reading the galley proofs of another Big Bend book—one with two chapters in it on Hallie—when he got the telephone call that she had died.

I saw Hallie for the last time in the spring of 1996. Linda and I wanted our Hallie to meet Hallie the elder, and vice versa. We finally got that done one Sunday afternoon at the Stillwell Ranch. The two-year-old and ninety-eight-year-old got along just fine.

"She's a real live wire," the elder Hallie said of her energetic namesake. So was she.

The younger Hallie was too little to know that she was meeting someone famous, but we shot video and took plenty of photographs. We want our Hallie, who has her own autographed copy of her namesake's book, to be able to say someday that "Hallie Stillwell was the only woman I knew who killed a mountain lion."

Here's to Your Health

Galloping Consumption

When the Texas Medical Association convened for its thirty-fifth annual meeting in San Antonio in the spring of 1903, one of the physicians who came to the Alamo City to present a paper to his professional colleagues was Dr. W.T. Jones of Fort Davis.

Standing before many of his fellow practitioners, Jones said that he had been asked to "prepare a paper upon the climate of Fort Davis, especially as regards tuberculosis." Having lived in the mile-high town for three years, the doctor declared that he had "no ax to grind" in that he did not operate a sanatorium for the treatment of TB patients, back then more commonly referred to as "lungers" suffering from "galloping consumption" (so known for the rapid wasting that preceded death).

While TB is known to have plagued humans for thousands of years, the condition—which in the nineteenth century led to one in seven of all deaths—had not been formally named until 1882, when Dr. Robert Koch's discovered *tubercle bacillus*. With the development of antibiotics still decades in the future, the prevailing medical belief in the early twentieth century was that, as Dr. Jones put it, "a moderately high altitude that is dry, and changes of temperatures not too great or sudden, is the ideal climate for [TB] patients."

Pointing to the fact that the U.S. Army had a TB sanitarium and hospital at Fort Bayard, New Mexico, a cavalry post standing at 6,040 feet above sea level, Dr. Jones noted that Fort Davis lay at the foot of the Davis Mountains 5,200 feet above sea level. Residents enjoyed mild winters and relatively cool summers in the low humidity of the high country, he said.

In fact, the doctor continued, compared with "some of the most noted resorts in the world"—including Denver, Colorado; Pensacola, Florida; Asheville, North Carolina; Venice, Italy; Bordeaux, France; and San Diego, California—Fort Davis had the lowest variance between mean summer and winter temperatures, only 18.7 degrees as compared with a 35.0-degree variance in Venice. In other words, Fort Davis tended to have moderate temperatures year round. On top of that, the doctor said, on average Fort Davis had only five cloudy days during the winter months, compared with thirty-four cloudy days in Augusta, Georgia. Finally, Fort Davis had the lowest mean relative humidity—33 percent compared with 77 percent in Augusta.

"I am fully convinced that a large percent of tuberculosis patients if sent to West Texas when the disease is in its incipiency, would recover, provided they were placed under proper case and treatment, and remain a sufficient length of time," he said.

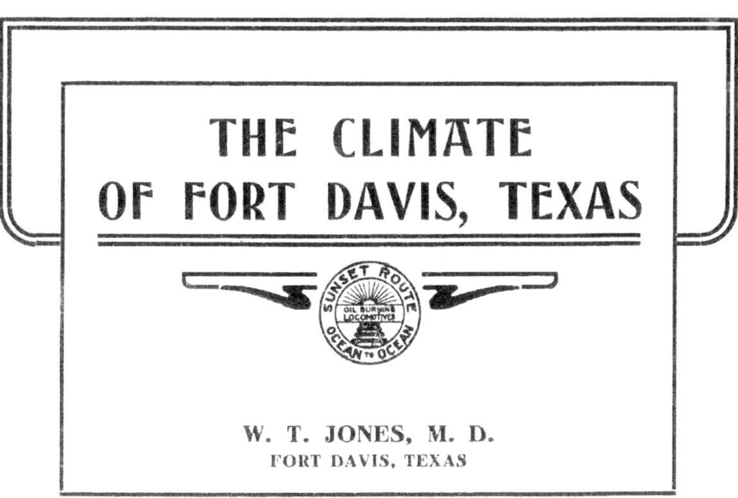

The Southern Pacific Railroad picked up the tab for Dr. W.T. Jones's booklet on the healthfulness of Fort Davis.

By way of example, Jones cited the case of a young woman who had come to Fort Davis two years earlier "with a well defined case of incipient tuberculosis of lungs, having high evening temperature, night sweats, distressing caugh and rapidly losing flesh [weight]." Those symptoms persisted, he continued, for eight to ten months before she started to get better. "She has had no elevation of temperature for nearly one year, coughs but little, very few bacilli in sputum, and now weighs 162 pounds—more than she ever weighed," he added.

How a patient spent his or her time in high climate had as much to do with their recovery as the altitude, the doctor said. "A very grave error, committed by some physicians when sending tuberculosis patients to this or any high altitude, is the advice to rough it, and take all the exercise possible," Jones lectured. "I have been told by some, that their physicians had instructed them to go to the mountains of West Texas, camp out, drink whiskey and rough it."

Admitting that a few patients did survive "the ill effects of such pernicious advice," Dr. Jones said, "the great majority succumb sooner or later to the rapid progress of the disease, superinduced by exposure, over exertion and excessive indulgence in whiskey—most likely the latter."

The Fort Davis doctor's advice was for absolute rest until the patient became acclimated, followed by "gentle exercise" once their temperature had normalized. Though he cautioned that the high altitude of Fort Davis was not good for those who suffered heart disease, it was a great destination for those with asthma, hay fever, rheumatism and "all malarial troubles."

Jones ended his paper with a gentle call to action. "Could our law makers and wealthy philanthropists be aroused to the urgent necessity, and be induced to build and maintain consumptive sanitariums in this healthful region…many human lives would be saved, the lives of many more materially prolonged, and the spread of 'the terrible white plague'…would greatly diminish."

Within a few years, Jeff Davis County did have a privately operated tubercular sanitarium in Grape Canyon, east of the town. But it was not the type of facility that Dr. Jones had envisioned. Known locally as "Tent City," the camp featured a frame structure that served as a combination dining and recreation hall and a dozen residences with adobe walls and canvas roofs. The operation folded within a few years.

The medical association published the doctor's talk along with all of the other papers presented at that year's San Antonio conference. The paper also saw distribution, with nine photographs of various Fort Davis scenes, as a twenty-four-page booklet, *The Climate of Fort Davis, Texas.* Jones had said that he had no axe to grind in advocating Fort Davis as the site of a sanatorium, but the last page of the booklet offers as a clue about those who did have an interest in the town's development as a destination for TB sufferers—that page is an advertisement for the Sunset Route, predecessor of the Southern Pacific Railroad.

The railroad's Sunset Express (later called the Sunset Limited) passed through nearby Marfa twice daily, and it was only a twenty-two-mile stagecoach ride from there to wellness at Fort Davis.

Flora's Tree

The giant pecan, which still stands outside of Helen Bentley's house in Fort Davis, grew from a sapling planted in 1873.

While the tree has long since exceeded a pecan's typical seventy-five to one-hundred-year lifespan, some pecans have been known to live for two centuries or more. But the exceptional age of the huge tree in Fort Davis is only part of its story, a tale that begins with the arrival of a mulatto Buffalo soldier at the army garrison that gave this mile-high community its name.

That soldier was Kentucky-born George Bentley, a private who came to Fort Davis in April 1868 with Company K, Fifth U.S. Infantry. Then twenty-three, he had enlisted in the army at Louisville, Kentucky, on December 8, 1866. Though he and his fellow foot soldiers left Fort Davis for occasional marches in the field, his primary duty was baking bread. In May 1871, the army moved Company K farther west to Fort Quitman on the Rio Grande in what is now Culberson County, but when his enlistment expired that December, Bentley returned to Fort Davis and got a job as a civilian packer and teamster. Now married, Bentley also acquired some cattle, there still being plenty of free grazing land available.

"My pa had cattle by the time he quit the army," George Bentley Jr. told writer Barry Scobee in the spring of 1964. "One day he was looking after them down Limpia Canyon when he saw a little bitty pecan switch growing out of the ground by some boulders where there was a water seep."

The former soldier, not realizing that the Davis Mountains did have a small population of native pecans, wondered how the sapling got where it did. "He said likely soldiers, or maybe Indians, rested in the shade of the rocks and dropped a pecan that germinated," Bentley told Scobee.

Less interested in the sapling's origin than its potential to provide shade and pecans for his growing family, Bentley plucked the sprout and brought it home with him. "My sister Flora, oldest of the seven children, planted it close to a well that was twelve feet deep and in rich soil," Bentley said. With ample moisture and nutrients, the sapling took root and grew into a sturdy tree. After about a decade, the pecan began producing nuts, the robustness of its yield cycling every other year.

While even a hearty tree can fall victim to disease, in the days before penicillin and more sophisticated antibiotics, children were particularly vulnerable to dangerous infections. One of the cruelest diseases was diphtheria, a highly contagious upper respiratory disease often caused by bacteria in unpasteurized milk. Victims experience sore throats, raging fevers and increasingly impaired breathing as a membrane grows across the trachea. Eventually, death comes from suffocation.

In the fall of 1891, within a span of two horrible weeks, the Bentleys teenage daughter Flora and six of her siblings were dead of diphtheria. Bentley and his wife buried their children at Pioneer Cemetery, a graveyard begun in the 1870s and used up until 1914. Dr. I.J. Bush, newly arrived to Fort Davis, had treated the children, but there was little he could do. One by one, they died terribly, their helpless parents incapable of intervention.

Bush later told Scobee that he had never seen such a serious outbreak of the disease. "People died like flies," the doctor recalled in a letter to Scobee sent in 1936, "including the Bentley children, who ranged in age from two months to seventeen years."

As if burying their children was not hard enough on the grieving parents, a vicious rumor made the rounds that the deaths had come as fulfillment of a curse that had been placed on Bentley for bayoneting an Apache infant while in the military, an allegation not supported by any known record.

Since his beloved daughter Flora had planted the tree in the yard, Bentley took to calling it Flora's Tree. In time, the couple's anguish waned. They went on to have three more children, including George Bentley Jr., born in 1902.

By the time the story of the tree came to Scobee's attention, the old pecan had grown to a circumference of eight feet, four inches. Its branches extended so far that some of them had to be propped to keep them from breaking. In good years, it produced some two hundred pounds of pecans.

Mysteries

A Mountain Mystery

Letting his horse do the thinking, the man held the reins lightly as the animal worked its way up the narrow mountain trail, steam blowing from its nostrils in the cold fall air. The scabbard holding his rifle bounced against the horse's flank as the rider scanned the granite boulders above for any movement. Hoping for a big-racked mule deer, he knew that he also might jump a mountain lion or black bear.

The hostile Indians who had necessitated the presence of Fort Davis had long since been subdued, and word was that the army intended to abandon the garrison. But while the danger of getting scalped had passed, the Davis Mountains in the late nineteenth century remained wild and remote. They also offered good hunting.

Suddenly the man stopped his horse and raised his black field glasses to take a better look at something farther up the rocky, winding trail. It was a cabin, but the hunter knew of no habitations this high up in the mountains. Hoping whoever lived there might have a pot of coffee on the stove, the rider slowly moved closer.

When his horse stepped from the trail onto the small, level shelf where the cabin stood, the man yelled out a friendly "Hello!" When no one answered after a respectful period of time, the man dismounted and walked slowly toward the open door of the frame cabin.

Inside, though everything lay covered in dust, it looked like whoever had lived here had departed expecting to come right back. Crumpled newspapers dated many years before plugged cracks to keep out wind and cold. A long-barreled rifle hung from wooden hooks on the wall. A table in the center of the shed remained set with china. The potbellied stove still held ashes. Kindling was piled nearby. A water bucket rested on a shelf. In the corner, an unmade bed looked like someone had just crawled out of it.

Hearing running water, the hunter stepped out the back door of the cabin and found a faucet turned wide open. Looking up, he saw a pipe running down from what must be a spring about a hundred feet farther up the mountain. Clearly, whoever had lived here had put the water to good use. The occupant had put in a small garden. Beets and assorted herbs pulled from the soil lay nearby, well-preserved in the dry desert.

Half expecting to find an equally mummified corpse, the hunter moved from the cabin to a shed behind it. That's when he saw something that just didn't make sense: an old buckboard. The trail leading to the cabin could barely accommodate a horse, much less a wagon.

"How did this man manage to get it to such a place?" a newspaper writer would later ask rhetorically after listening to the hunter's story of his strange high country discovery. "Of what earthly use could it have been in these rough and rugged mountain heights, where even if men get around at all, he must crawl or leap from crag to crag…this rude vehicle could not be drawn through these mountains by either man or beast."

After studying on it for a while, the hunter concluded that the man who had lived here either had found or blazed a road to the cabin that he could not now find, or the man had hauled the wheels and other parts up the mountain piece by piece on the backs of pack mules and then reassembled the components. But again, unless there was some other way out of here, that made no sense.

The hunter built a fire in the stove, laid his own bedroll on the bed and passed a comfortable night, even though it took him a while to fall asleep as he pondered who had built the cabin and why.

Back in Fort Davis a few days later, he started asking around until he finally found someone who knew about the cabin and its one-time occupant. Visiting Austin the following summer, the hunter related the tale to a reporter for the *Austin Statesman*, which ran the story, "Davis Mountain's Tale," on July 24, 1905.

Years before, A.D. Stanton, a wealthy man from Montpelier, Vermont, came to Fort Davis for his health. Having plenty of money, he hired laborers to haul lumber and supplies up one of the highest mountains in the area and built a twelve- by twelve-foot cabin that took up about 25 percent of the ledge on which it stood. Stanton furnished the cabin with "simple though comfortable furniture, which included books and writing material, a good supply of provisions, then dismissed his force of laborers and moved in," the article related.

For three years, folks said, Stanton lived a hermit's life in the cabin. He had picked a spot so high that on some days a layer of clouds below would obscure his otherwise spectacular view of the surrounding country. He spent his time reading, gardening and, doubtless, in reflection.

And then one day he realized that he felt better than he had in years. To his mind, the high, dry climate had healed him. Knowing that some day he might want or need to return, he left most of his things behind and traveled back to New England.

"It may be remarked that nothing has ever been heard of Mr. Stanton since he left his mountain home many years ago," the newspaper article concluded, "except one time when he wrote an acquaintance that his health was good, and that he hoped his Davis mountain cabin would not be disturbed."

Unfortunately for history's sake, in addition to not identifying the hunter who stumbled upon the cabin, the writer of that piece did not name the mountain where that cabin stood or who owned the property. What became of Stanton, and whether any evidence of the cabin survived into the twenty-first century, remains a mystery.

The Wonderful Boy

His father a respected Uvalde County rancher, the quiet, good-looking Guy O. Fenley seemed like a typical teenager except for one thing—newspapers called him the "wonderful boy…with X-ray vision."

One night in 1896, Joel Fenley had been walking in one of his pastures with Guy tagging along. "Look at that stream of water," the boy said excitedly to his father. The elder Fenley knew his property. They were nowhere near any water. But the boy insisted that he saw flowing water—underground.

Back home, Fenley filled a wooden bucket with water, had his son go into another room and then placed the bucket under a wooden table. Dousing the lights, he led the boy back into the room and asked him to point to the spot on the table corresponding with the bucket below. The boy did.

Soon after, Fenley asked his son to show him again where he had "seen" the underground water. Fenley hired a driller and hit water at 167 feet.

Word of the boy's supposed visual acuity began to spread, but most folks had a hard time believing it. That doubt began to erode when people heard what happened on the Thomas Devine Ranch. After walking around for a couple of hours, Fenley excitedly said that he had found flowing water about 175 feet down. The boy indicated several locations where he said water lay near the surface. Each spot produced a well.

In January 1901, early during that year's legislative session, Alpine Representative Wigfall Van Sickle had a conversation with Uvalde Representative John Nance Garner about the trouble he had been having trying to find water on his Big Bend ranch. The future vice president suggested that Van Sickle get in touch with one of his constituents, Joel Fenley. Word had it that Fenley's son could see underground water.

While that sounded far-fetched, both legislators knew that some people did seem able to find water with willow divining rods. Hoping that young Guy was one of those so-called water witches, Van Sickle invited the Fenleys to Alpine to see if the boy could help him.

Van Sickle had already sunk $1,500 into a 607-foot dry hole on his Glass Mountains ranch. In short order, the boy identified two points where he said water would be found. Both resulted in wells. Guy reportedly also found water on the previously dry Big Bend ranches of two uncles.

Not long after visiting Alpine, Fenley's story broke nationally. First appearing as a letter from someone in Austin to the *St. Louis Globe-Democrat*, the story ran in the *Galveston News* on February 9, 1901. The article noted that Guy had recently been offered $500 to find water on F.K. Moore's ranch in Edwards County. He refused to take any money for his services, but he found water on the place.

An editor in Galveston had asked the newspaper's Austin correspondent to check with Garner about the boy's reputed gift. The journalist wired back: "He says it is not a fake. He knows the boy personally, and has seen him locate water underground. Whether he has 'X-Ray' eyes or not Mr. Garner does not presume to know, but he says the facts related are true."

Others have claimed X-ray vision over the years, but they have never successfully demonstrated their powers to scientists using standard experimental protocols. In the case of more high-profile claimants, one common factor appears to be an association between their power and the receipt of something of value for their services. But no evidence has turned up that Fenley or his family ever tried to capitalize on "the wonderful boy's" supposed ability.

In the early 1900s, the media loved to perpetrate or at least circulate hoax stories, from tales of petrified giants to people with superpowers. Most of those tended to be created from whole cloth, but Guy Fenley was a real person from a no-nonsense, well-thought-of Texas family. His relatives did not know how he did what he did, but they believed him.

In the spring of 1901, a reporter for the *San Antonio Express* interviewed Joel Fenley. "I can no more explain it than anybody else," the teenager's father said. "I have thoroughly tested the matter and am convinced that the boy can see as he says. I am naturally adverse to anything connected to claims of supernatural power or of a superstitious nature and would not believe my son's statements until he convinced me of its truth by many demonstrations."

Then the newsman asked Fenley if he could speak with his son privately. The father agreed. Describing the boy as "averse to talking about his visual endowments," the journalist managed to get this quote: "I don't know…I can just see the water, just like you can see something in the street out there. That's all I know about it. I just see it, that's all."

When he grew up, Fenley took up ranching in Zavala County, where he later served as a county clerk. Whether his power continued or waned went unreported. He died in 1968 at seventy-nine.

While mainstream researchers insist that no real science lies behind the claims of those who say they can find water beneath the ground, more than a century after "the wonderful boy" made national headlines, Guy Fenley's purported power remains unexplained.

El Viejo Gringo

> *OLD, adj. In that stage of usefulness which is not inconsistent with general inefficiency, as an* old man.
>
> –*Ambrose Bierce,* The Devil's Dictionary

Aside from *The Devil's Dictionary*, his best-known book, Ambrose Bierce's greatest work was the final chapter of his own life story.

That he figuratively scripted his last act, or at least its opening scenes, is supported by the well-documented fact that he took literary license in telling about his early life. In his 2004 essay "Ambrose Bierce and the Joy of Outrage," Ohio University English professor, author and bibliophile Jack Matthews pointed out that Bierce had lied to biographer (and friend) Walter Neal about his place of birth, "claiming it was in Ohio's Western Reserve, thus giving emphasis to his proud New England ancestry, but in doing so, missing his actual birthplace by 200 miles." In truth, Bierce was born near Horse Cave Creek in Meigs County, Ohio. Bierce did at least own up to the correct date, which was June 24, 1842.a

But anyone with even modest skills at prevarication can falsify his place of birth. Plotting the end of one's life takes a bit more work. And Bierce did it as only a longtime professional writer could. "His exit from the theatre of life was strikingly melodramatic, a triumph of stagecraft," Matthews continued. "It was...splendidly theatrical...and it has been the inspiration for films and books, along with much speculation."

Bierce, a physically and emotionally scarred Civil War veteran who went on to become one of the nation's best-known, if acerbic, journalists and short story writers, got the last part of his story moving by deciding to travel to Mexico and participate in the ongoing Mexican Revolution. How much further he went in crafting the resolution of his story remains a mystery, but it came to a close somewhere near or in the Big Bend.

The beginning of the final arc in Bierce's storyline came in December 1911 when he attended the funeral of his friend, Percival Pollard. Four years earlier, the two men had toured the Civil War battlefields of Tennessee

Writer Ambrose Bierce joked about ending up in front of a Mexican firing squad before he disappeared in 1913.

Painting of Ambrose Bierce.

together before traveling to Galveston for a boozy vacation. For Bierce, Pollard's death came as the latest in a depressing string of personal losses. The journalist's seventeen-year-old firstborn son had killed himself in 1889; his only other son died of pneumonia or acute alcohol poisoning (or both) in 1901; and his ex-wife had died in 1905.

In June 1912, the month he turned seventy, Bierce traveled from Washington for what proved his final visit to his adopted home state of California. Less than a year later, he began planning a trip to Mexico. "I mean to go into Mexico—where, thank God, something is doing," he wrote his friend and future biographer Walter Neal on May 29, 1913. The "something...doing" was the vicious warfare wracking northern Mexico.

On October 2, 1913, Bierce wrote a letter to his niece that had the metaphoric thumbprints of a man contemplating the end of his life all over it. "Dear Lora," he began, "I go away tomorrow for a long time...Good-bye—if you hear of my being stood up against a Mexican stone wall and shot to rags please know that I think that a pretty good way to depart this life. It beats old age, disease, or falling down the cellar stairs. To be a Gringo in Mexico—ah, that is euthanasia!"

By October 24, after spending some time revisiting other Civil War battlefields, where he had seen fierce action half a century earlier, Bierce reached New Orleans. There, a newspaper reporter quoted him as saying, "I'm on my way to Mexico because I like the game."

Four days later, Bierce was honored at a dinner thrown at Fort Sam Houston in San Antonio. Maybe some of his friends in the military arranged for a similar reception at Laredo's Fort McIntosh, which he visited on or about November 6. "[I] don't know where I shall be next," he wrote his niece. "Guess it doesn't matter much. Adios."

From Laredo, Bierce continued by train westward across the Big Bend to El Paso, where on November 28, 1913, he crossed into Juarez, Mexico, on a rented horse. Some sources say that he had $2,000 in gold on him.

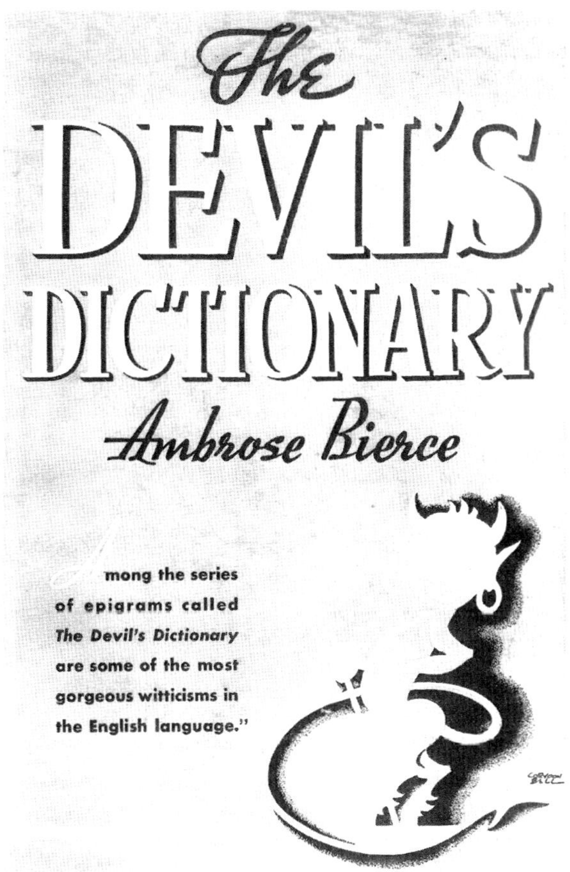

Where the man who compiled *The Devil's Dictionary* ended up remains a mystery.

Bierce succeeded in his plan to connect with Francisco (Pancho) Villa, then fighting federal forces for control of Chihuahua. From the state capital of Chihuahua City, Bierce posted his last known letter the day after Christmas. That missive went to Carrie Christiansen in Washington, his secretary (and, apparently, lover), with the report that he anticipated leaving with Villa's force the following day for Ojinaga, the Mexican town across from Presidio, Texas.

Villa's troops took control of Ojinaga in early January 1914, but no evidence has been found to support that Bierce, who seems never to have needed much excuse to take a drink, participated in the victory celebration. That's because he was either dead or about to be.

The basic scenarios, in order of the credibility accorded them by scholars, are: a) Bierce died violently in the fighting (the principle subsets being robbery-murder by bandits or in front of a firing squad after encountering federal soldiers not impressed with his literary renown); b) he died of disease, asthma being the most likely cause, but stress-induced heart failure a definite possibility; or c) that he took his own life.

"The most rational explanation for the disappearance of Bierce is that he came north with Villa, arrived near Ojinaja on January 9, [1914] and was either slain during the battle on January 10 or that he died of natural causes sometime during that…time frame," wrote Big Bend writer-historian Glenn Willeford in his essay, "Ambrose Bierce, 'the Old Gringo': Fact, Fiction and Fantasy."

The second level of the mystery is the location of Bierce's final resting place. Bierce had been to Marfa at least once, when he traveled by rail to El Paso. And in the early 1990s, the story arose that he might be there still, at least his remains.

In 1992, Dr. Earl Elam, a professor at Alpine's Sul Ross State University and editor of the *Journal of Big Bend Studies*, interviewed a man named Aberlardo Sanchez of Lancaster, California. Sanchez told Elam that in 1957 he had been driving in northern Mexico and had picked up an older man who said he had fought against Villa at Ojinaga. When the border city fell, he and several thousand other soldiers and their families escaped across the Rio Grande into Texas. During that frantic exodus, he encountered a gravely ill gringo whose first name sounded something like "Ambrosia." The man's last name he heard as something like "Price." The Mexican told Sanchez that he and some other soldiers had transported the old man across the river in a two-wheeled cart. Troops of the Third Cavalry then escorted the refugees and the sick American to Marfa. Delirious by the time they reached Marfa, the elderly gringo died soon thereafter and was buried in the Camp Marfa cemetery.

But Elam could find no civil or military record listing such a death of anyone with a name even remotely similar to Bierce's on or about the date in question. Of course, recordkeeping is never perfect during the chaos of war, and the military later exhumed those buried in the post cemetery at Marfa for reinterment at the National Cemetery in San Antonio. The public cemetery where he also could have been buried had to be moved a few years later due to erosion.

Most likely, the writer who preferred bypassing old age if possible got his wish, ending up in an unmarked grave somewhere on the Mexican side of the river.

The Man Under the Black Fedora

Doing research for his master's thesis on the history of a trading post that operated in a remote part of the Big Bend from the mid-1920s through mid-1940s, former Upton County sheriff Glenn Willeford paged through the guest register owner Elmo Johnson had kept. One of the signatures suddenly caught his attention.

Six entries up from the bottom of page 105 was "John Dillinger… Chicago." The signature bore no date, but it came after an entry dated March 24, 1934, and before another signature dated April 1, 1934.

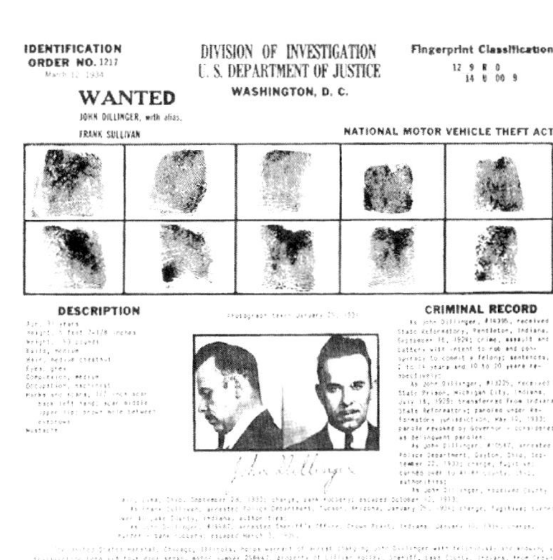
IDENTIFICATION ORDER NO. 1217
March 12, 1934

DIVISION OF INVESTIGATION
U. S. DEPARTMENT OF JUSTICE
WASHINGTON, D. C.

Fingerprint Classification
12 9 R 0
14 U 00 9

WANTED
JOHN DILLINGER, with alias,
FRANK SULLIVAN

NATIONAL MOTOR VEHICLE THEFT ACT

DESCRIPTION

CRIMINAL RECORD

A historian and former Texas peace officer believes that Public Enemy No. 1 John Dillinger might have hidden out in the Big Bend for a while.

More than likely, Willeford thought, someone who had come to the Rio Grande to fish or swim in the river on Johnson's ranch thought it would be funny to put the notorious outlaw's name in the book. It sure wouldn't be the first time in history someone had scribbled a phony signature in a guest register.

Willeford knew the rough outline of Dillinger's story, including the fact that he had broken out of jail by using a wooden gun to threatened his guards and had remained at large for several months before the FBI finally tracked him down and killed him. But he didn't know the exact dates.

Checking Robert Cromie's *Dillinger: A Short and Violent Life*, Willeford found that Dillinger had escaped from jail in Crown Point, Indiana, on March 3, 1934. The outlaw with the big smile and little mustache had last been seen six days later in Chicago, and his whereabouts had remained unknown until agent Bob Purvis gunned him down in front of Chicago's Biograph Theater on July 22.

Assuming that the FBI had a copy of Dillinger's signature on a fingerprint card, Willeford sent the bureau's crime lab a photocopy of the register page from 1934 for comparison on July 8, 1993. Within the month the lab reported that the known Dillinger signature did not match the questioned signature.

"One argument against the handwriting being Dillinger's," Willeford had said in his letter to the bureau, "is that some people feel he would not have wanted anyone to know where he was. Conversely, it may be argued that the outlaw wanted to leave the impression he was going into Mexico in order to throw his pursuit off track."

Judging from a page-one article in the April 9, 1934 issue of the *El Paso Herald-Post*, the FBI either had information or at least suspected that Dillinger might be trying to get into Mexico. "Dillinger," the article said, "is believed traveling this way in a Ford deluxe sedan or coach bearing Minnesota license plate B4-20-213." The outlaw's description and the plate number had been broadcast over the El Paso Police radio station.

While Willeford had not been the first person to notice the Dillinger signature on the guest register, he was the first researcher to try to prove or disprove its authenticity. One motivating factor was his awareness that there had been talk for years that Dillinger had spent some time in the Big Bend while on the lam.

On November 17, 2010, Willeford interviewed Shirley Rooney of Marathon, a seventy-six-year-old widow born barely a month after Dillinger's violent demise. Her parents had attended school at Balmorhea, and when she was a little girl, her folks went there every summer for a family reunion. They'd gather at Toyahville, an even smaller community about two miles from Balmorhea. Nearby was an old tourist court adjacent to Phantom Lake called Splitgarber's, a collection of small frame cabins dating to the 1920s operated by Charles Splitgarber.

Like most reunions, the ones held by her clan saw plenty of storytelling. Some of those stories got told year after year, especially one that her dad liked to tell. Mrs. Rooney repeated it for Willeford:

> *One day at Crenshaw's Grocery…these two black hardtop sedans* [others remembered the vehicles as an Auborn and a Cord] *rolled into Balmorhea. They came from the west and they stopped there at Crenshaw's. There was two women with 'em. And about four-five men. The women would get out and go into the store and buy groceries like bread and meat.*

The men would get out of the cars and stand around while the women did the shopping:

> *They had dark three-piece suits and fedora hats like they wore then. My dad said they didn't speak to anybody, they didn't bother anything, but they were looking around constantly standing right there by those two cars. As soon as the ladies would get there with the groceries, they'd get back in the cars and head back west again. Of course being a small town, the rumor said they were staying in the Splitgarber's cabins.*

Rooney told Willeford that the visitors stayed around Balmorhea for about a month. "Then one morning they were just gone," she said.

When Dillinger got killed in Chicago, his photograph and pictures of his other gang members appeared in all the newspapers. That's when people in Balmorhea realized who their low-key visitors had been—Dillinger and his gang. Others said that they saw the outlaw and his associates in Pecos, where they had their vehicles serviced at the Justis Garage and shopped at the Leader Grocery.

"That's all I know about the story, but I know that it was a true story because my parents and grandparents had no reason to joke with me about it," Mrs. Rooney said. "My dad always said that was Balmorhea's fame, having the Dillinger gang there."

Duncan Kingston, another Big Bend old-timer, recalled before his death in 1978 that a well-dressed party of vacationers had stayed at Splitgarber's in the early 1930s. He remembered two couples and a pretty woman who seemed to be a third-wheel, "Miss Green."

Kingston believed that he was making progress in talking her into a date when the visitors suddenly left town. He heard from Splitgarber that they had said they had to attend to some "financial matters" but would be back. When they returned, the young woman agreed to go out with Kingston. But before that could happen, the out-of-towners disappeared again. Not long after that, Kingston saw a photograph of "Miss Green" in the newspaper. Only she was "Mrs. Green," widow of the late Eddie Green, a member of Dillinger's gang shot to death by police in late March 1934.

Despite the FBI's assertion that the signature submitted by Willeford did not match Dillinger's known signature, the cop turned history detective was not totally convinced. Studying photographs of the trading post in its heyday, Willeford noted that the register "Dillinger" signed stood low enough to have caused whoever signed the book to do so at an angle that could have affected their handwriting.

Bryan Burrough's *Public Enemies*, published in 2004, has information on Dillinger from then newly opened FBI files. One revelation was that when Dillinger made his break in Indiana, he freed an inmate with whom he had become friends. On the way out, the man started to grab one of several wool overcoats hanging on the wall inside the jail.

"Where we're going, you won't need one," Dillinger supposedly said.

Willeford thinks that Dillinger and company may have headed south to the Big Bend, possibly contemplating crossing the river into Mexico. But if he did come to Texas, he changed his mind and went back to his old stomping grounds, a fatal mistake.

Chronicles

Before Twitter, "Coo-er" Carried the News

Decades before "tweet" would take on new meaning and "Twitter" became a proper noun, an innovative newspaper writer-photographer used a different kind of tweeter—well, maybe "coo-er" would be a better word—to communicate from the desolate reaches of the Big Bend.

Wilfred Dudley Smithers, far better known as W.D. Smithers, was born in 1895 in San Luis Potosi, Mexico, where his father kept the books at an American-owned mine. His family had moved to San Antonio in 1905. As a teenager he got interested in photography, taking his first pictures in 1912 and, a year later, building his own camera. Smithers first saw the Big Bend in 1915 while serving as an army teamster. In 1917, he joined the cavalry but soon became involved in military aviation, teaching aviators aerial gunnery and helping to pioneer aerial photography. Both as a teamster and later as a soldier, he took numerous photographs in the Big Bend, producing a rich archive of images chronicling almost every aspect of the region and its people.

Honorably discharged in 1919, Smithers traveled in Mexico for a time and did more pack animal work in the Big Bend before moving to San Antonio in 1920. There he operated a photography studio until 1929. During that time, he wrote for the *San Antonio Light*. He also made frequent trips to the part of Texas he found most interesting, the still wild Big Bend. The only problem with covering news in such a remote area was timely communication.

In the late fall of 1928, Smithers drove to the Big Bend to shoot photos for the *Light* and explore the area for stories. To get his dispatches back to San Antonio from locales lacking even post offices, not to mention telegraph service or telephones, he brought with him eight carrier pigeons loaned by Arthur Ward of San Antonio. One of them, a blue scale cock known only as No. 749, held the national carrier pigeon speed record.

In the truest tradition of owner William Randolph Hearst, the *Light* hyped Smithers's trip as if he were headed to darkest Africa. "Armed with three cameras and [eight] carrier pigeons," the newspaper reported on November 22, "[Smithers] is on his way [to] the unexplored Big Bend territory of Texas." At least the newspaper admitted this was Smithers's sixth trip to that "rugged portion of the country" so far that year. According to the story, Smithers planned to take photos from the tops of Mount Ord and Cathedral Mountain, to visit a Texas Ranger camp at Glenn Springs (scene of a bloody bandit raid thirteen years earlier), to do some horseback exploration at Rancho Valle de la Cienga and the Stillwell Ranch and to "snap" Governor Dan Moody when he visited Santa Helena Canyon in early December. Finally, he hoped to take pictures of "Uncle" Jim McMahon, "aged trapper [who] is known the length of the Rio Grande, making the dangerous Santa Helena and Boquillas rapids in his small boat."

While apparently a first for the San Antonio daily, using pigeons to send messages was not a revolutionary new idea. Pigeons that repeatedly proved that you can go home again had been used extensively during World War I and, to some extent, in earlier conflicts. England first learned of the outcome of the Battle of Waterloo via pigeon, and the birds had been used for communication long before that, all the way back to ancient Egypt. But so far as was known, Smithers was the first to use carrier pigeons in the Big Bend.

Smithers's first dispatch, a short news item written by chamber of commerce secretary Mrs. W.B. Hamilton, the *Light*'s Alpine correspondent, arrived in the Alamo City on November 26. Thanks to its winged messenger, the eighty-three-word report may have reached San Antonio in a hurry, but the news it contained wasn't likely to knock a subscriber's hat off:

> *Alpine's big school bond issue was definitely decided upon and the school board will call the bond election Dec. 10, according to Mr. J.E. Wright, president of the Brewster County chamber of commerce. This important step was taken at a meeting of the C. of C. public improvement committee*

> *held jointly with the school board today. Plans submitted by Page and Page, Austin, for the reconstruction of the old plant and the construction of a new University high school building were unanimously approved.*

A pigeon carrying a second message from Smithers arrived at the residence of its owner on the morning of November 30. "Bird Brings 2d Message to *Light*," the newspaper proclaimed on page one of its December 2 edition. The bird had made the 450-mile trip, a route that including navigating over more than five-thousand-foot mountains in twenty-four hours. (Pigeons are known to fly fifty miles per hour or more, so if it took a full day for it to get to San Antonio, the bird must have taken some time for sightseeing.) Smithers's report noted:

> *Near trading post Castolon. Been having car trouble. Lots of rain and plenty cold. Getting good pictures. Will try to make it to Glenn Springs tonight. Not much signs of the road since the rains yesterday. Too many hawks, so didn't send bird. Will have six birds left.*
>
> *Went on* [mountain] *lion hunt. Got two and pictures. Saw lots of game and hunters but not in right places. Talked to a man who said wild pigeons in Chisos Mountains, but have no proof of it. Approximately 450 miles to San Antonio.*

Curiously, the *Light* made no further mention of its Big Bend carrier pigeon service after that second report. The newspaper may have chosen to tone down its promotion of Smithers's use of pigeons after hearing that Mexican liquor smugglers operating through the Big Bend had threatened his life, wrongly thinking that the photographer was using the birds to snitch on them. Or maybe Smithers's pigeons flew the coop, having realized that they were expected to fly over mountains and risk predators for mere bird feed.

What became of Smithers is better documented. Finally moving to Alpine in 1935, Smithers produced and sold photographs and photographic lamp shades. In the early 1950s, he began writing about the Big Bend and his experiences. He stayed in Alpine until 1974, when he relocated to El Paso. He died poor and with no next of kin on June 24, 1981, at the Veteran's Hospital in Albuquerque, but he left a rich legacy of photography and writing, without which much less would be known about the Big Bend.

J. Frank Dobie in the Big Bend

It's not mentioned in any of his biographies, but one of Texas's best-known authors wrote portions of one of his best-known books while sequestered in a tarpaper-covered shack in the Chisos Basin.

J. Frank Dobie, raised in the flat brush country of south Texas and schooled in humid central Texas at Georgetown's Southwestern University, first saw the high, dry Big Bend country in 1910 when he got off the train at Alpine. Fresh out of college, he had been hired to teach English at Alpine High School. Being the only male faculty member, he also—at twenty-two—would be the school's principal.

Dobie's letters to his future wife, Bertha, reveal that while he didn't like the isolation of the small west Texas ranching town, he did appreciate that he had come just about as close to what remained of frontier Texas as he would ever get. While in Alpine, where he lived in a boardinghouse, he became acquainted with John Young, an old south Texas cowboy. Though schooled in the classics, the young teacher-headmaster enjoyed listening to old-timers like Young hold forth on their adventurous salad days.

After classes ended in the spring of 1911, Dobie got offered a teaching job at his alma mater's prep school back in Georgetown and quickly accepted it. While the rancher's kids he taught probably ended up knowing more about English poetry than they thought useful, the payoff for Dobie's Alpine stint proved to be his association with Young, which in 1929 culminated in his first book, *A Vaquero of the Brush Country*.

Producing a succession of books after that, including the bestselling collection of treasure stories he called *Coronado's Children*, by the late 1930s Dobie had become a Texas icon. And in 1938, he signed a contract to produce a book on another Texas icon, the longhorn.

In January 1939, Dobie holed up for a time at the four-year-old Civilian Conservation Corps camp in the Chisos Basin, the future heart of Big Bend National Park. While CCC men blazed trails, graded roads and built infrastructure, Dobie worked to cobble together earlier longhorn stories he had written while also adding new material for a work that would bear the simple title of *The Longhorns*.

What little is known of Dobie's stay in the Big Bend may be credited to Fred Gipson, then a roving columnist for Texas's Harte-Hanks newspaper chain. Gipson, who while a student at the University of Texas had taken Dobie's popular southwestern literature course, probably remembered

Dobie better than Dobie remembered him. A successful if typically low-paid journalist, Gipson still chafed at the suggestion that Dobie had made after reading some of his work at UT: don't figure on a career as a writer.

Nevertheless, the affable, white-haired writer graciously greeted Gipson at the door of the CCC structure he had been living in. "Come into this house," he said, taking Gipson's hand in both of his. Inside, the air was thick with Dobie's pipe smoke.

"How's the Texas longhorn book coming?" Gipson soon asked. He saw paper in a typewriter on a small table and a clutter of notes on a bigger table nearby.

"I'm just this minute chasing a longhorn bull over a ridge," Dobie said. "But sit down and tell me about yourself. I don't think that bull will get away for a little bit."

They rolled cigarettes and talked. After the smokes, Dobie led Gipson outside for a commentary on the magnificent peaks circling the basin. Even though he had come there to write about a notable breed of Texas cattle,

J. Frank Dobie wrote parts of his classic book on Texas longhorns while holed up in the Chisos Basin.

Dobie seemed constitutionally incapable of visiting a place without acquiring information and stories about its people, animals and features.

On their way back to the shack, Dobie stopped at the ample woodpile stacked nearby. "Like to chop wood," he said, "nearly as well as I like to ride a horse. When my mind doesn't work good, I come out and chop wood… See, here's a piece of mountain ebony."

The temperature fading with the sun, Dobie started a fire in the cabin's wood heater. Needing to do some writing of his own, Gipson hauled in his portable typewriter, and both men hit the keys as night came. By the time Gipson finished a column, fine snow had begun falling. Dobie had already quit for the day and had gone down to park caretaker Lloyd Wade's cabin to see about supper.

As Gipson drove to Wade's cabin to join them, the headlights of his car stopped a mountain lion slinking in a nearby arroyo. The big cat looked at the car for a minute but then ambled off into the darkness.

The visiting reporter, Dobie, Wade and Tom Mercer, a Texas Railroad Commission inspector based in San Angelo, sat on rough benches to a meal of chili con carne, frijoles and fried potatoes. Afterward, as the wind howled and the snowflakes grew bigger, the men talked of cattle and cowboys. It was nearly midnight before they got the last old longhorn rounded up and went to bed.

Dobie's 1941 book still stands as the starting place for anyone interested in Texas longhorns, but Dobie was not incapable of misjudgment. Ignoring his former professor's pronouncement that he'd never make it as a writer, Gipson went on to produce one of the world's enduring children's classics, *Old Yeller.*

Low Man on the Totem Pole Comes to Alpine

Something about the mountainous vastness of the Big Bend attracts colorful characters. I first came to understand that one afternoon sitting in the newsroom of the *San Angelo Standard-Times*, some 250 miles east of the Big Bend. But in 1967, the morning edition of that newspaper covered a hunk of west Texas larger than Ohio. The Big Bend lay well within our circulation area.

Managing Editor Dale Walton—the tall, thin, chain-smoking, coffee-swilling man who had hired me—came up and asked if I had ever heard of H. Allen Smith. I had not. Walton told me that Smith was a famous New

York humorist who had started off as a newspaperman. Smith had recently been a guest on NBC's *Today Show*, and while being interviewed about his latest book, *Son of Rhubarb*, he had revealed that he had bought a "place" near Alpine, Texas, and might move there next year. When asked what he didn't like about New York, Smith had answered, "People and things."

Before talking to me, Walton had taken a call from Alpine justice of the peace Hallie Stillwell, our correspondent for that area. She had told him about Smith's plans to relocate to the Big Bend. Walton handed me a page of typewritten notes he had taken while talking to Stillwell, told me to add some background on Smith and wrap it up into a story about him moving from the Big Apple to the Big Bend. As soon as I could, I walked from the newspaper plant to the nearby Tom Green County Library, looked up Smith in *Who's Who* and checked out Smith's *Low Man on the Totem Pole*, his 1941 memoir about his early days as a newspaperman. Being low man on the totem pole on the San Angelo newspaper, that night I started reading the book with a more than casual interest. I wanted to write books someday, too.

Humorist H. Allen Smith's "Mount Corpus Christi." In a typical Smith-style gag, he proposed moving this mountain from Alpine to the Texas coast.

The result of this was a story headlined "Noted Author Plans Move from New York to Alpine" that ran the next morning with an Alpine dateline followed by "(SC)," the newspaper's way of saying the piece came from one of its "Special Correspondents" even though I had written it.

While my name did not appear on that story, that fall I did have a couple of bylined pieces about Smith's ongoing duel of words with *Dallas Morning News* columnist Frank X. Tolbert over the merits of midwestern chili versus Texas chili. Smith was an old hand at knowing how to say something that newspaper reporters would like, so getting enough material had been easy and fun.

Having picked a piece of real estate on the flank of a mountain looking down on Alpine, Smith finally moved to town during the Thanksgiving holiday. A few days later, I interviewed him by telephone. "I heard someone say the other day that direct distance dialing and H. Allen Smith were coming to west Texas soon," Smith cracked, "and no one knew which is going to cause the most confusion."

The following summer, I finally got to meet Smith in person. He and his wife had rented a small apartment in Alpine while their $90,000 mountainside home was under construction. I spent most of a Sunday afternoon with him, lapping up every word he said along with the Coors beer he graciously provided, even though I was still a year shy of my legal majority.

I knew Smith had moved to Alpine because he had grown tired of the rat race in New York, but I pumped him for more detail. "I was writing a book about a tour of the west [*We Went Thataway*, 1949], and we passed through Alpine," he recalled. "I stopped the car on the other side of town and said to my wife, 'Did you notice that town?' She said, 'What town?'"

Smith turned around and checked into the Holland Hotel. "My god, they didn't even have any motels then." They stayed in Alpine for two days. When they headed east for Del Rio, he had two notebooks full of notes about assorted Big Bend people. "Everyone I met was a character."

As the conversation and the beer flowed, I filled up a small pocket-sized notebook and then started on some paper he gave me. I was interested in getting material for a good newspaper feature, but looking back at my notes, it's clear that I was also picking his brain about writing. After all, Smith had started his successful book-writing career as a newspaperman, and I aspired to do the same thing.

Despite all of the notes I took that afternoon, when I got back to San Angelo I wrote to Smith asking him a few more questions. (During my interview, he had told me that his mentor, H.L. Mencken, liked to say that a gentleman always answers his mail, so I knew he'd respond.) On August 6, 1968, Smith dashed out a six-sentence letter to me, noting he was late in answering my questions because he'd been away in Santa Fe.

"My advice to beginning writers would be to read history and biography until it is running out of their ears," he offered. Even so, he concluded, "It is my opinion that writers are born and cannot be taught to write."

After I left the San Angelo newspaper, I didn't have as much contact with Smith, though I reviewed several of his books when they came out and began to collect his older books. In 1972, I had another long interview with him on another trip to Alpine. By this time, he had been in his house overlooking the town for years. That was the last time I ever talked with him. Fortunately, for posterity's sake, I have our conversation on tape.

After moving to the Big Bend from the Big Apple, author H. Allen Smith sent his friends this Christmas card to prove that he had become a Texan.

At the time, I worked for the afternoon newspaper in Austin. Every weekday, shortly before noon, someone carried a hot-off-the-press stack of the first edition into the newsroom and plopped it down on the slate-gray copy desk. I'd grab a copy and read it at my desk.

That's what I was doing on February 25, 1976, when a headline caught my interest: "Humorist dead at age 69." The four-paragraph wire service brief that followed noted that H. Allen Smith, "American newspaperman, author and humorist whose irreverent pokes at humanity enlivened more than three decades," had died of a heart attack in a San Francisco hotel room the day before.

Fittingly, given Smith's aversion to overpopulated places, his wife had her husband's ashes scattered over the rocky Big Bend mountainside he had chosen as his last home.

About the Author

Mike Cox, an elected member of the Texas Institute of Letters, is the author of twenty nonfiction books. After nearly two decades as an award-winning journalist, he began a long career as a state employee, first as a spokesman for the Texas Department of Public Safety, then as communication manager for the Texas Department of Transportation and currently, following a short-lived retirement, as a spokesman for the Texas Parks and Wildlife Department. He lives in Fredricksburg in the Texas hill country.